THE AMERICAN SERIES

of

FOREIGN PENAL CODES

17

THE SWEDISH PENAL CODE

THE PENAL CODE OF SWEDEN

As Amended January 1st, 1972

Originally
Translated by

Thorsten Sellin
University of Pennsylvania

Amendments Translated by
Jerome L. Getz, Esq.

Introduction by

Lennart Geijer
Minister of Justice

FRED B. ROTHMAN & CO.
SOUTH HACKENSACK, N.J.

SWEET & MAXWELL LIMITED
LONDON

1972

Published in the U.S.A.
by Fred B. Rothman & Co.
of 57 Leuning Street
South Hackensack N.J.

Published in Great Britain
by Sweet & Maxwell Limited
of 11 New Fetter Lane
London Law Publishers

Printed in the U.S.A.
by
Edwards Bros. Ann Arbor, Michigan.

ISBN NO. 0-8377-0037-X

Editor-in-Chief

GERHARD O. W. MUELLER

THE AMERICAN SERIES OF FOREIGN PENAL CODES

1. THE FRENCH PENAL CODE, translated by JEAN F. MOREAU and GERHARD O. W. MUELLER, with an introduction by MARC ANCEL, 1960.
2. THE KOREAN CRIMINAL CODE, translated and with an introduction by PAUL K. RYU, 1960.
3. THE NORWEGIAN PENAL CODE, translated by HARALD SCHJOLDAGER and FINN BACKER, with an introduction by JOHS. ANDENAES, 1961.
4. THE GERMAN PENAL CODE, translated by GERHARD O. W. MUELLER and THOMAS BUERGENTHAL, with an introduction by HORST SCHRÖDER, 1961.
5. THE TURKISH CODE OF CRIMINAL PROCEDURE, translated by the LEGAL RESEARCH INSTITUTE, the NEW YORK UNIVERSITY FACULTY TEAM, the JUDGE ADVOCATE'S OFFICE OF THE JOINT UNITED STATES MILITARY MISSION FOR AID TO TURKEY, WILLIAM BELSER, YILMAZ ALTUG and TUGRUL ANSAY, edited by CHARLES TENNY and MUSTAFA T. YÜCEL, with an introduction by FEYYAZ GÖLZÜKLÜ, 1962.
6. THE ARGENTINE PENAL CODE, translated by EMOLIO GONZALEZ-LOPEZ, edited by FREDERICK W. DANFORTH, JR., with an introduction by RICARDO LEVENE, h. 1963.
7. THE FRENCH CODE OF CRIMINAL PROCEDURE, translated and with an introduction by GERALD L. KOCK, 1964.
8. THE JAPANESE DRAFT PENAL CODE, 1961, with an introduction by JUHEI TAKEUCHI, 1964.
9. THE TURKISH CRIMINAL CODE, translated by the JUDGE ADVOCATE'S OFFICE OF THE JOINT UNITED STATES MILITARY MISSION FOR AID TO TURKEY, *et al.*, with an introduction by NEVZAT GÜRELLI, 1965.
10. THE GERMAN CODE OF CRIMINAL PROCEDURE, translated by HORST NIEBLER, with an introduction by EBERHARD SCHMIDT, 1965.
11. THE GERMAN DRAFT PENAL CODE E1962, translated by NEVILLE ROSS, with an introduction by EDUARD DREHER, 1966.
12. THE AUSTRIAN PENAL ACT, translated by NORBERT D. WEST and SAMUEL I. SHUMAN, with an introduction by ROLAND GRASSBERGER and HELGA NOWOTNY, 1966.
13. THE ISRAEL CRIMINAL PROCEDURE LAW, with an introduction by U. YADIN, 1967.
14. THE COLOMBIAN PENAL CODE, translated and with an introduction by PHANOR EDER, 1967.
15. THE SWEDISH CODE OF JUDICIAL PROCEDURE, translated and with an introduction by ANDERS BRUZELIUS and RUTH BADER GINSBURG, 1968.
16. THE GREENLAND CRIMINAL CODE, translated at the CENTER FOR STUDIES IN CRIMINAL JUSTICE, UNIVERSITY OF CHICAGO LAW SCHOOL, with an introduction by VERNER GOLDSCHMIDT, 1970.
17. THE SWEDISH PENAL CODE, translated by THORSTEN SELLIN, amendments translated by JEROME L. GETZ, with an introduction by LENNART GEIJER.

in preparation

ARGENTINE MODEL CODE OF CRIMINAL PROCEDURE

GREEK PENAL CODE

ITALIAN PENAL CODE

SPANISH PENAL CODE

PUBLICATIONS OF THE COMPARATIVE CRIMINAL LAW PROJECT

Vol. 1. ESSAYS IN CRIMINAL SCIENCE (Mueller, ed.), by 17 authors from 8 nations, 1961.

Vol. 2. INTERNATIONAL CRIMINAL LAW (Mueller & Wise eds.), An Anthology, 1965.

Vol. 3. THE GENERAL PART OF THE CRIMINAL LAW OF NORWAY, by JOHANNES ANDENAES, 1965.

Vol. 4. JAPANESE CRIMINAL PROCEDURE, by SHIGEMITSU DANDO, transl. by B. J. GEORGE, JR., 1965.

Vol. 5. THE EFFECTIVENESS OF PUNISHMENT, by WOLF MIDDENDORFF, 1968.

CONTENTS

Part Three. Of Sanctions

PREFACE

No member of the late Professor Joseph Loman's graduate Criminology course at the University of Chicago in the academic year 1950–51, is likely to forget a session in which a distinguished visitor reported to the class on his recent visit to Sweden, his first post-war visit. The distinguished visitor, none other than the great criminologist, Thorsten Sellin, spoke of concepts in Swedish practice which to us appeared to be little more than pipe dreams for the rest of the world: A reduction of retributive justice, abolition of the cellular system of imprisonment, introduction of the day fine system, useful employment for convicts, in short, a system devoted to the preventive and rehabilitative ideals, the system of social defense.

In the years that followed, Thorsten Sellin kept the American professional public informed about Swedish developments in criminal justice, and all of us came to know of the masters of the Swedish system of criminal justice, among whom Karl Schlyter, Birger Edeberg, Nils Beckman, Sten Rudholm and Ivar Strahl, ranked foremost. In 1965 the cooperation of Professors Ivar Strahl of the University of Uppsala and Thorsten Sellin of the University of Pennsylvania led to the translation and publication of the new Penal Code of Sweden, effective January 1, 1965, which is reflective of all the modern thinking of which the generation of giants of Swedish criminal justice and criminology had been capable. The Code was widely heralded all over the world, and it met with success at home. As with any piece of legislation, the need for improvement and amendments became apparent from the day of its promulgation. Consequently, the first six years after its enactment witnessed numerous amendments, which necessitated the publication of an up-dated and amended version of this Code. We have obtained the gracious permission of the Royal Ministry of Justice to base our translation on the original text, and His Excellency, Lennart Geijer, Royal Minister of Justice, has kindly provided us with an Introduction explanatory of the experiences under the Code since 1965, and of the amendments enacted since then. In view of the facts that the original edition was published so recently and was distributed so widely, and that an English-language textbook on Swedish Penal Law (Nelson, Responses to Crime) is now available, the editors did not deem it advisable to reproduce the original Introduction to the Code, although it is clear that any serious student would wish to consult that Introduction.

The editors want to express their deep appreciation to all those who labored on this Code and nand its English translation before them, particularly Professors (Emeriti) Ivar Strahl and Thorsten Sellin. But their gratitude includes those who devoted much time and attention to the current edition, including His Excellency Lennart Geijer, for his superb Introduction, Jerome L. Getz, Esq., for his basic translation, Mr. Gerard Ferguson for his editorial labors and our secretaries Carol Maxfield and Tsige Haimanot for their secretarial help. Last, but not least, our gratitude is due to all our students in our joint post-graduate seminar of Comparative Criminal anal Law at New York University, 1971, who participated in making the Swedish experience applicable to American conditions and who thus contributed significantly to the completion of this volume of the American Series of Foreign Penal Codes.

Alvar Nelson		Gerhard O. W. Mueller
Uppsala, Sweden	1971–72	New York, New York

Introduction

A new penal code came into force in Sweden on January 1, 1965. This Code, which superseded the earlier Penal Code of 1864, was the result of many years of work on the reform both of the provisions concerning specific offences and the system of sanctions. In some respects the rules in the new Penal Code, called Brottsbalken in Swedish, are only a transposition of the penal provisions in force at the time that the Code was introduced. In other respects, especially so far as the system of sanctions is concerned, the Penal Code contains important innovations.

The introduction of the new Penal Code has not meant that reform of penal law has stopped. Development in this matter has not come to a halt over questions of what shall be punishable, how serious a given offence shall be considered to be or what measures shall be taken about the offender. The legislator must always be prepared not only to amend the law so as to reflect public opinion, but also, when necessary, to guide development in a given field.

The continuing work of reform has already led to several important changes in the Penal Code. Reforms are also planned which will concern both the rules relating to specific offences and to the system of sanctions. A short account of these changes, together with proposed reforms, is now given.

1. In order to extend the rights of freedom of speech and of demonstration, amendments have been made in, inter alia, *Chapters 5, 16* and *19*. A special committee appointed to review the legislation on freedom of speech and freedom of the press presented proposals in 1969 for amendments, inter alia, to the rules of the Penal Code concerning incitement to rebellion, breach of religious peace and offences against morality and decency. The proposals, after some revision, led to a rule concerning impunity in petty cases of incitement to rebellion (*Chap. 16, Sect. 5*). The provision concerning breach of religious peace (*Chap. 16, Sect. 9*) was abolished on the ground, among other reasons, that religious persons or groups enjoy protection of their faith and its practice through other provisions in the Penal Code, such as Chap. 16, Sections 4 and 8. In addition the provision concerning offences against

morality and decency was superseded by a rule on punishment for forbidden dealing in pornographic pictures (*Chap. 16, Sect. 11*). This amendment rests on the view that a person who wishes to view pornography should decide this for himself but, on the other hand, no one should be forced against his will to be faced with pornographic representations which, according to a widespread opinion, may be regarded as an offence against morality or offensive to a sense of propriety. It was considered urgent to break the trend in recent years towards an increasingly uninhibited dissemination of exceptionally daring pornographic products among persons who do not wish to take note of them. Only certain forms of dissemination of pornographic representations have therefore been made punishable through the new rule. Otherwise all pornography, written and pictorial, has been freed.

Concurrently with these legislative measures other amendments were introduced, chiefly in order to extend the freedom of speech in connection with demonstrations. It was pointed out in this connection that demonstrations are a valuable complement to other means for influencing opinion and that the right of demonstration should not be subject to restrictions other than those that seem necessary having regard to other important national interests. It therefore appeared desirable to review the offences relating to freedom of speech which acquire a particular importance in connection with demonstrations. This review led to the rule mentioned above concerning impunity for petty cases of incitement to rebellion (*Chap. 16, Sect. 5*) and to the abolishment of the provisions concerning the penalty for insulting a Swedish or foreign national symbol (*Chap. 16, Sect. 7,* and *Chap. 19, Sect. 10*). The provisions were no longer considered to fulfill any real function. Certain special rules concerning prosecution and punishment in cases of offence against the Head of State or representative in Sweden of a foreign power were also amended (*Chap. 5, Sect. 5, Chap. 19, Sect. 11 and 16*).

2. In some cases amendments have been made by reason of Sweden's accession to international conventions. The UN Convention on the Elimination of All Forms of Racial Discrimination has led to an extension of the provisions of *Chap. 16, Sect. 8,* which deal with agitation against an ethnic

group, to cover categories other than those which were earlier protected thereby. The definition of what is punishable under this clause has been extended in other respects as well. As well as threat, every expression of disrespect for a particular ethnic group has been made a criminal offence. The prerequisite for what is considered public has been extended so that a penalty can be imposed, for example, for the dissemination of culpable announcements among the public through repeated statements in private conversations. As well as the provision concerning agitation against an ethnic group, a provision concerning a new crime called unlawful discrimination, has been introduced in *Chap. 16, Sect. 9,* the section which previously dealt with breach of religious peace. For this new crime a penalty can be imposed, for instance, on a tradesman who exercises racial discrimination in his business.

Another convention to which Sweden has acceded and which has led to amendments of the Penal Code is the Convention for the Suppression of Unlawful Seizure of Aircraft. A new provision has been introduced in *Chap. 13, Sect. 5 a,* concerning sanctions for seizure of aircraft. Furthermore, through an amendment of *Chap. 2, Sect. 3, point 4,* Swedish courts have been given jurisdiction over such offences regardless of where or by whom they are committed.

3. For a long time the Nordic States have been cooperating in different ways to bring about greater uniformity in Nordic legislation. Originally, this was concerned chiefly with civil legislation, but since the end of the Second World War considerable attention has also been given to the question of uniform penal legislation. This has led to uniform legislation concerning extradition for crime and enforcement of a sentence imposed in a criminal case in another Nordic country.

As far as the Penal Code is concerned the joint Nordic work on legislation has led to amendments of the rules concerning release on parole in *Chap. 26* and concerning forfeiture in *Chap. 36.* One of the reasons for the amendment of the rules concerning release on parole was the desire to eliminate certain differences between the laws of the Nordic countries and thus to avoid difficulties in the application of the Nordic enforcement laws. Under this legislation a sentence of imprisonment in one Nordic country can under certain circumstances be enforced in another Nordic country. Another reason for the amendments was the view that, on grounds of criminal policy, release on parole should constitute an element in the treatment of the sentenced person to a greater extent. As a result of the amendments the compulsory form of release on parole after serving five-sixths of the term of imprisonment was abolished. Instead, a discretionary form of release on parole after two-thirds or—if special reasons exist—after one-half of the term has been served, was introduced. Certain changes where also made concerning the right of decision on questions of release on parole and the length of the parole period. In 1970 a permanent Penal Law Committee (which had been appointed in 1960 with representatives from all Nordic countries), presented proposals concerning certain minor amendments to *Chap. 26* of the Penal Code in order to attain further uniformity between the countries for the treatment of persons released on parole. The proposal is at present under examination within the Ministry of Justice. It may be added that the Penal Law Committee has recently been instructed to investigate whether release on parole, to a greater extent than at present is possible, can be allowed after the serving of only half of the period of imprisonment.

For *Chap. 36* too, one of the main aims of the amendments was to facilitate cooperation between the Nordic countries in respect of enforcement of sentences, including those involving forfeiture of property. In *Chap. 36 Sections 1–4 and 9–12* have been amended.

4. The basic provisions for the protection of both tame and wild animals is to be found in *Chap. 16, Sect. 13.* An amendment, implying a greater stringency, has been made in this section in that the word "undue" now refers to the act which has given rise to the suffering. A greater attention can thus be paid to the disposition of the perpetrator and the intention of the act.

5. An important function in the non-institutional correctional system is performed by the supervisory boards. Rules concerning their composition etc. are contained in *Chap. 37, Sections 1 and 2.* A minor alteration to these rules now permits the rapid appointment of a temporary deputy for the chairman of such a board to take place.

6. A large number of the amendments made in the Penal Code are consequences of new or amended legislation in other fields. Under new legislation introduced in 1965, government and municipal employees acquired, in principle, the same right as other employees to negotiate with their employer over their conditions of employment, work and pay. Their salaries can, and to a large extent are, regulated by collective agreements. This bargaining right also implies that civil servants have the right to take part in strikes arranged by their trade union against the Government or local authority. On the other hand the Government and local authorities, as employers, may have recourse to lockout against their employees. Both forms of action have been taken. As a result of the 1965 legislation, *Chap. 20, Sect. 4* and *Chap. 21, Sect. 18* were amended so that a civil servant or permanently employed member of the Armed Services cannot be penalized for breach of official duty on account of having participated in a strike decided on by a trades union.

Because of the lowering of the age of majority from 21 to 20 years, the corresponding age limits in *Chap. 6, Sections 4, 7 and 8,* have been altered. The 21-year age limit in the system of sanctions for young offenders, e.g. in *Chap. 26, Sect. 4,* and *Chap. 29, Sect. 1,* has however been retained.

A new law on improper marketing was introduced in 1970. Under this law a penalty may be imposed on a tradesman who, in the marketing of a product or service, intentionally uses a misleading description. This penal provision was considered entirely to cover the field embraced by *Chap. 9, Sect. 8, second sentence,* which was therefore deleted when the new law entered into force. In 1970 a new law on the protection of registered designs and a law amending the law on copyright were introduced. In this context the term "applied art" was introduced in place of "artistic craftsmanship," which necessitated an editorial amendment in *Chap. 14, Sect. 5.*

Chap. 30, Sect. 7, and *Chap. 31, Sect. 3,* concerning mentally abnormal offenders, have been amended to comply with the new laws concerning the provision of institutional psychiatric care and the care of certain mentally retarded persons.

Through amendments which entered into force on January 1, 1971, a uniform organization of the lower courts was introduced and, in conjunction with this, the rules concerning competence of a lower court were amended. This reform necessitated amendments in *Chap. 38, Sect. 6.*

A new law on special service, as an alternative service for recognized conscientious objection to National Military Service, entered into force in 1966. This necessitated amendments to *Chap. 21, Sect. 20.* The special service is in principle performed outside the Armed Forces and anyone undertaking it is not considered as a member of the Armed Forces. Such a person is not therefore subject to the penal regulations applying to a member of the Armed Forces.

Finally it may be mentioned that new legislation on the procedure within administrative authorities has recently been issued. The provisions of *Chap. 37, Sect. 6,* on the procedure in certain cases in the boards referred to in the same Chapter, have been amended to comply with the new legislation.

7. During the spring of 1971 the Government presented proposals to Parliament concerning certain alterations in *Chapters 2* and *35.* Owing to the similarity of legislation in the Nordic countries it was suggested that the requirement of special examination of the right of prosecution for a crime committed abroad should cease to apply to an act committed in another Nordic country (*Chap. 2, Sect. 5, point 3*). It was also proposed, on the basis of a proposal made by the aforementioned Nordic Penal law Committee, that the rules concerning time-limitation be so amended that a provision concerning extension of the term of limitation be abolished (*Chap. 35, Sect. 5*) and certain times of limitation be shortened (*Chap. 35, Sections 5, 6 and 8*). It is expected that the proposal will be discussed by Parliament during the autumn of 1971. This edition contains the proposed new wording of the sections.

The Government has proposed to Parliament during its 1971 autumn session that, as a general principle in regard to certain legal aspects, adopted children shall be considered as the children of those who adopt them and not as the children of their biological parents. In consequence it is proposed to abolish certain provisions concerning adopted children in a number of laws. Among these are *Chap. 5, Sect. 5, Chap. 8, Sect. 3 and 13* and *Chap. 17, Sect. 11* of the Penal Code.

8. Certain amendments of *Chapters 4, 8, 9, 10, 16* and *32* are at present being considered within the Ministry of Justice. A committee for the investigation of questions concerning stricter protection of the right to privacy has proposed a new provision in *Chapter 4* imposing a penalty for unlawful eavesdropping. Under the proposal a person shall be punished who unlawfully introduces technical equipment for reproduction of sound in another person's dwelling and certain other locations, as well as a person who, with such equipment, unlawfully listens to or records what takes place in such locations. *Chap. 4, Sect. 11,* is also affected by the proposed amendment. Another committee, which is investigating the question of the procedure for hearing of cases relating to certain minor offences, has issued a report concerning, among other things, the penal status of petty theft and proposals for action against shop-lifting. The committee considers that penal measures should be limited and imprisonment abolished for certain minor offences against property. It is proposed that the penalty for petty theft (*Chap. 8, Sect. 2*), fraudulent conduct (*Chap. 9, Sect. 2*) and petty embezzlement (*Chap. 10, Sect. 2*) should be limited to a fine. This would have a considerable effect on the procedure for dealing with these offences. As regards shop-lifting the committee considers that this form of crime should be countered primarily by measures within shops. When cases of shop-lifting are prosecuted, the committee proposes the introduction of a prosecution rule particularly directed to cases of first offence. It is suggested that the rule be introduced in *Chap. 8, Sect. 13* and so formulated that, if petty theft relates to goods offered for sale in such a way that they are freely accessible or otherwise easy of access to the customer, it shall not be prosecuted unless so required by general considerations.

As regards *Chap. 16,* an amendment is being considered to *Sect. 13* concerning cruelty to animals, and abolishment of the provision in *Sect. 15* concerning punishment for drunkenness.

So far as cruelty to animals is concerned, the intention is to investigate whether the sphere of application of the penal provisions should be extended to cases not only in which the perpetrator has acted with intention but also to cases in which a person has subjected animals to suffering through negligence.

The proposal for the abolishment of *Chap. 16, Sect. 15,* was made by a committee appointed to investigate the modalities for dealing with persons in an intoxicated state in a public place. The committee considers that the present arrangement whereby the police take them in charge together with the punishment of acutely intoxicated persons, represents an antiquated attitude. It is pointed out that, from the medical standpoint, acute intoxication is to be regarded as an illness. The committee proposes that acute-clinics be established for the sociomedical treatment of intoxicated persons and that the penalty for drunkenness be discarded.

Finally, mention should be made of a committee for the investigation of penal and disciplinary measures against members of the Armed Services which has proposed amendments to *Chap. 32,* chiefly in order to reduce the use of military arrest. One proposal is that a new form of penalty should be introduced, a so-called leisure-time penalty.

9. Several committees are reviewing various aspects of the Penal Code and in certain cases this may result in amendments in the near future. A general review of the legislation on abortion is being made by a committee appointed in 1965 which is expected to submit a report later this year. The committee's proposals may affect the rules concerning abortion in *Chap. 3, Sect. 4.* The committee mentioned above on the review of legislation on freedom of speech and freedom of the press is continuing its work on revision of the rules governing defamation offences in *Chap. 5.* Under its terms of reference the committee will review the provision in *Sect. 4* concerning the penalty for defamation of a deceased person. A committee which is investigating the question of official liability and disciplinary liability in public service is expected later this year to submit a report which may lead to a radical revision of *Chap. 20* on crimes in office. In a report submitted earlier the committee proposed that the present official liability be abolished and that the penalties of suspension and dismissal be eliminated. The committee will later consider the question of liability for the taking of bribes by employees both

in public and private service. The question of the abolishment of enforcement of fines (*Chap. 25, Sect. 7 second paragraph*) is under study by a committee which is expected to conclude its work later this year. Mention is also made of the fact that the Nordic Penal Law Committee is currently investigating the possibility of extending the sphere of application for the rules in *Chap. 33, Sect. 3,* which concern deduction of the period on remand in custody, and of establishing similar rules in this respect within the Nordic countries.

10. The continued work on revision of the Penal Code is being conducted in accordance with earlier plans through partial reforms. The terms of reference have recently been drawn up for a review of sanctions for mentally abnormal offenders. The committee which is to examine this matter is, according to its terms of reference, to consider, among other things, whether the limitations in *Chap. 33, Sect. 2,* on the choice of sanction for the mentally abnormal should be retained. The provision is considered to lead to a certain rigidity in the system of sanctions and to complicate forensic psychiatric examination. *Chap. 31, Sect. 3,* which contains rules for the imposition, inter alia, of institutional psychiatric care, is also to be reviewed. A basis for the deliberations concerning these two clauses is that, in accordance with the current values prevailing in criminal policy, the choice of sanction should rest exclusively or preferably on a consideration of the mental state and social situation of the sentenced person at the time of prosecution. Another task for the committee is to consider whether greater scope should be left for altering a sentence while treatment is in progress.

The Ministry of Justice is also considering the setting up of a committee to review the rules concerning sexual offences (*Chap. 6*). Among the rules which may be particularly considered are those on homosexuality (*Sect. 4* and *8*), incest (*Sect. 5*) and procuring (*Sect. 7*).

In conclusion I may mention that the Ministry of Justice is also considering certain alterations of the Penal Code by reason of Sweden's intention to ratify a Convention drawn up within the Council of Europe, and already signed by Sweden, concerning the International Validity of Criminal Judgments. The Convention creates the means by which a criminal judgment can be enforced in another contracting State than that in which the judgment was pronounced. One condition for enforcement under the Convention is that the act to which the judgment relates is also punishable under the legislation of the State which is requested to enforce the sanction. The Convention also regulates the question of the legal effects of a foreign criminal judgment. According to the principle *ne bis in idem* these rules give a foreign judgment, whether acquittal or a sanction which has been enforced, the same *res judicata* effect in principle as a national criminal judgment. The implied principles, concerning the requirement of dual criminal liability and the effect of *ne bis in idem,* may necessitate changes to open the way for Swedish ratification of the Convention.

Stockholm, October 1971

Lennart Geijer
Minister of Justice

THE SWEDISH PENAL CODE

Issued At Stockholm's Castle, December 21, 1962

And As Amended Till January, 1972.

We, Gustavus Adolphus, by the grace of God King of the Swedes, the Goths and the Wends, make known that We, together with Parliament, have decided that there be introduced in the Statutes of the Swedish Realm, immediately after the Commercial Code, a new code, called the Penal Code, formulated as follows:

Part One

General Provisions

CHAPTER 1

Of Crimes and Sanctions

Sec. 1. Crime is an act for which a punishment as stated below is provided by this Code or by other codes or laws.

Sec. 2. Unless otherwise stated, an act described in this Code shall be regarded as a crime only if it is committed intentionally.

If the act has been committed during self-induced intoxication or if the actor had otherwise himself brought about the temporary loss of the use of his senses, this shall not cause the act to be considered non-criminal.

Sec. 3. A sanction for crime in this Code means:

the common punishments of fine and imprisonment;

the punishments of suspension or dismissal of a person exercising a function carrying official responsibility, and disciplinary punishments for members of the armed services; as well as

conditional sentence, probation, youth imprisonment, internment, and surrender for special care.

Sec. 4. The use of punishments is regulated, in general, by the statutory provisions governing the individual crimes. Other sanctions may, according to what is provided for their use, nevertheless be applied albeit they are not mentioned in those provisions.

Imprisonment, suspension, and dismissal are to be regarded as heavier sanctions than a fine and disciplinary punishments.

Sec. 5. Unless otherwise provided several sanctions for the same crime may not be imposed.

Suspension or dismissal are imposed collaterally with the sanction to which it is found that the accused should be sentenced.

Sec. 6. Unless otherwise provided, a joint sanction for the crimes shall be imposed when someone is to be sentenced for several crimes.

If there are special reasons for it, a person may be sentenced for one or more crimes to pay a fine together with a sanction for additional criminality, or to imprisonment together with conditional sentence or probation for the rest of his criminality.

Sec. 7. In the choice of sanctions, the court, with an eye to what is required to maintain general law obedience, shall keep particularly in mind that the sanction shall serve to foster the sentenced offender's adaptation to society.

Sec. 8. Aside from a sanction, and in accord with appropriate statutory provisions, a crime can incur forfeiture of property or some other special consequence defined by law and may also incur liability for the payment of damages.

CHAPTER 2

Of the Applicability of Swedish Law

Sec. 1. A person, who has committed a crime within this Realm, shall be tried according to Swedish law and in a Swedish court. The same applies when it is uncertain where the crime was committed but grounds exist for assuming that it was committed within the Realm.

Sec. 2. If a crime has been committed outside the Realm by a Swedish citizen or by an alien domiciled in Sweden, he shall be tried according to Swedish law and in a Swedish court.

If some other alien, while being outside the Realm, has committed a criminal act which was punishable under the law in force at the place of the crime, he shall be tried according to Swedish law and in a Swedish court, if, after having committed the crime, he has become a Swedish citizen or has acquired domicile in this Realm or if he is a Danish, Finnish, Icelandic, or Norwegian citizen and is found here, and similarly too if he is found in the Realm and the crime is punishable according to Swedish law by imprisonment for more than six months.

Sec. 3. Even in a case other than those mentioned in Section 2, an alien, who has committed a crime outside the Realm, shall be tried according to Swedish law and in a Swedish court:

1. if he committed the crime on board a Swedish vessel or airplane or if he was a commanding officer or belonged to the crew of such carrier and committed the crime while in that capacity;
2. if he committed the crime in an area where a detachment of military forces was found but, unless he was a serviceman, only if the detachment was there for other than training purposes;
3. if the crime was committed against Sweden, a Swedish citizen or a Swedish group, institution or organization or against an alien domiciled in Sweden; or
4. if the crime is aircraft hi-jacking or violates international law. As amended, SF5 1971:188, eff. June 9, 1971.

Sec. 4. A crime is deemed to have been committed where the criminal act occurred and also where the crime was completed or, in the case of attempts, where the intended crime would have been completed.

Sec. 5. Prosecution for a crime committed within the Realm on a foreign vessel or airplane by an alien, who was a commanding officer or belonged to the crew of or otherwise accompanied the carrier, against such alien or a foreign interest shall not be instituted without an order from the King or from someone authorized by the King to give such order.

Prosecution for a crime committed outside the Realm may be instituted only pursuant to an order as stated in the first paragraph. Nevertheless, prosecution may be instituted without such order if the crime was committed:

1. on a Swedish vessel or airplane or, while on duty, by the commanding officer or some member of the crew of such carrier,

2. by a serviceman in an area where a detachment of the armed services was found,

3. in Denmark, Finland, Iceland or Norway or on a ship or aircraft in regular commerce between places located in Sweden or any of the aforesaid states, or

4. by a Swedish, Danish, Finnish, Icelandic or Norwegian citizen against a Swedish interest. As amended, SFS 1971:964, to be proclaimed effective on a date decided by the King.

Sec. 6. No one may, without an order from the King or from some one authorized by the King to give such order, be prosecuted for an act for which he has been subjected to punishment or other sanction outside the Realm. If prosecution is instituted in this Realm, the fixing of the sanction shall be done with due consideration for what he has suffered outside the Realm, and he may according to circumstances be sentenced to a lesser punishment than the one set by law for the act or be completely absolved of punishment.

Sec. 7. Aside from the provisions of this chapter regarding the applicability of Swedish law and the jurisdiction of Swedish courts, attention shall be paid to the limitations resulting from generally recognized principles of international law or, in accord with special statutory provisions, from agreements with foreign powers.

Sec. 8. Separate statutory provisions govern extradition for crime.

Conditions stipulated in connection with extradition from a foreign state to Sweden shall be complied with in this Realm.

Part Two

Of Crimes

CHAPTER 3

Of Crimes Against Life and Health

Sec. 1. A person, who takes the life of another, shall be sentenced for *murder* to imprisonment for ten years or for life.

Sec. 2. If, in view of the circumstances that led to the act or for other reasons, the crime mentioned in Section 1 is considered to be less grave, imprisonment for *manslaughter* shall be imposed for at least six and at most ten years.

Sec. 3. If a woman kills her child at its birth or else at a time when, due to her confinement, she is in a disturbed mental state or in grave distress, she shall be sentenced for *infanticide* to imprisonment for at most six years.

Sec. 4. A person, who with the aid of internal or external means unlawfully aborts or otherwise kills a foetus, shall be sentenced for *abortion* to imprisonment for at most two years. If such act has been performed by the woman herself the sanction may be remitted in her case if there are extenuating circumstances.

If an abortion committed by some one other than the woman herself is regarded as grave, the sentence shall be imprisonment for at least one and at most six years. In judging the gravity of the crime, consideration shall especially be given to whether the act was habitual or done for gain or had involved special danger to the woman's life or health.

Sec. 5. A person who inflicts bodily injury, illness or pain upon another or renders him unconscious or otherwise similarly helpless, shall be sentenced for *assault* to imprisonment for at most two years or, in case the crime was petty, to pay a fine.

Sec. 6. If the crime mentioned in Section 5 is considered grave, the sentence shall be for *aggravated assault* to imprisonment for at least one and at most ten years.

In judging the gravity of the crime, special attention shall be paid to whether the deed involved a mortal danger or whether the offender had inflicted grievous bodily injury or severe illness or had otherwise shown great ruthlessness or brutality.

Sec. 7. A person, who through carelessness causes the death of another, shall be sentenced for *causing another's death* to imprisonment for at most two years or, if the crime is petty, to pay a fine.

If the crime is grave, imprisonment shall be imposed for at least six months and at most four years.

Sec. 8. If a person through carelessness causes another to suffer bodily injury or illness not of a petty nature, he shall be sentenced for *causing bodily injury or illness* to pay a fine or to imprisonment for at most six months.

If the crime is grave, imprisonment for at most two years shall be imposed.

Sec. 9. If a person through gross carelessness exposes another to mortal danger or danger of severe bodily injury or serious illness, he shall be sentenced for *creating danger to another* to pay a fine or to imprisonment for at most two years.

Sec. 10. Attempt or preparation to commit murder, manslaughter, infanticide or an assault not of a petty nature, or attempt to commit abortion, also conspiracy to commit murder, manslaughter or aggravated assault or failure to reveal such crime shall be punished as stated in Chapter 23.

Sec. 11. In case of abortion or attempted abortion, the woman herself may not be subject to public prosecution unless such prosecution is deemed called for in the public interest.

Assault, which is not of a grave nature and did not occur in a public place, or attempt or preparation to commit such a crime, may be prosecuted by the public prosecutor only if the person aggrieved reports the crime for prosecution or prosecution appears called for in the public interest.

Causing bodily injury or illness may, if the crime is not grave, be subject to public prosecution only if the person aggrieved reports the crime for prosecution and such prosecution appears called for in the public interest.

CHAPTER 4

Of Crimes Against Liberty and Peace

Sec. 1. If a person seizes and carries away or confines a child or some other person with the intent of injuring him in body or health or forcing him into service, or to practice extortion, he shall be sentenced for *kidnapping* to imprisonment for a fixed period of at least four and at most ten years, or for life.

If the crime is less grave, imprisonment for at most six years shall be imposed.

Sec. 2. A person, who, in a case other than those stated in Section 1, deprives some one of his liberty by carrying him away or confining him or otherwise, shall be sentenced for *unlawful deprivation of liberty* to imprisonment for at least one and at most ten years.

If the crime is less grave, a fine or imprisonment for at most two years shall be imposed.

Sec. 3. A person, who otherwise, by unlawful compulsion or deceit, accomplishes the entry of some one into military or labor service or other similar condition of restraint or induces some one to go to or remain in a place abroad where he can be in danger of being exposed to persecution or exploited for immoral purposes or otherwise land in distress, shall be sentenced for *placing a person in a distressful situation* to imprisonment for at least one and at most ten years.

If the crime is less grave, a fine or imprisonment for at most two years shall be imposed.

Sec. 4. A person, who, by assault or otherwise by force or by threat of a criminal act, compels another to do, submit to or omit to do something, shall be sentenced for *unlawful coercion* to pay a fine or to imprisonment for at most two years. If some one with such effect exercises coercion by threat of prosecuting or accusing another of a crime or of giving detrimental information about another, he also shall be sentenced for unlawful coercion, provided that the coercion is wrongful.

If a crime referred to in the first paragraph is grave, imprisonment for at least six months and at most six years shall be imposed. In judging the gravity of the crime, special attention shall be paid to whether the act included the infliction of pain to force a confession, or other torture.

Sec. 5. If a person raises a weapon against another or otherwise threatens to commit a criminal act, in a manner suited to evoke in the threatened person a serious fear for his own or some one else's safety as to his person or property, he shall be sentenced for *unlawful threat* to pay a fine or to imprisonment for at most two years.

Sec. 6. A person, who unlawfully intrudes or remains where another has his living quarters, whether it is a room, a house, a yard or a vessel, shall be sentenced to pay a fine for *breach of domiciliary peace.*

If a person, without authorization, intrudes or remains in an office, factory, other building or vessel or a storage area or other similar place, he shall be sentenced for *unlawful intrusion* to pay a fine.

If the crime mentioned in the first or second paragraph is grave, imprisonment for at most two years shall be imposed.

Sec. 7. A person, who manually molests or by discharge of a firearm, throwing of stones, making loud noise or other heedless conduct harrasses another, shall be sentenced for *molestation* to pay a fine or to imprisonment for at most six months.

Sec. 8. If a person unlawfully obtains access to a communication which in the form of mail or as telephone conversation, telegram or other telecommunication is being transmitted by a public agency of communication, he shall be sentensed for *breach of postal- or tele-secrecy* to pay a fine or to imprisonment for at most two years.

Sec. 9. A person, who, in a case not covered by Section 8, unlawfully opens a letter or a telegram or otherwise obtains access to something kept safely under seal or lock or otherwise enclosed, shall be sentenced for *intrusion in a safe depository* to pay a fine or to imprisonment for at most two years.

Sec. 10. Attempt, preparation or conspiracy to commit kidnapping, unlawful deprivation of liberty or placing a person in a distressful situation, failure to reveal such a crime, as well as attempt or preparation to commit unlawful coercion of a grave nature shall be punished as stated in Chapter 23.

Sec. 11. Breach of domiciliary peace or unlawful intrusion not of a grave nature, molestation which did not occur in a public place, or intrusion in a safe depository may be prosecuted by the public procecutor only if the person aggrieved reports the crime for prosecution or when prosecution is called for in the public interest. The same applies to unlawful coercion by threat to prosecute or accuse another of crime or to give damaging information about another, as well as to attempt or prepare for such a crime.

CHAPTER 5

Of Defamation

Sec. 1. A person, who points out some one as being a criminal or as reproachable for his mode of life or otherwise gives information likely to expose him to the disesteem of others, shall be sentenced for *defamation* to pay a fine.

If he was in duty bound to express himself or if, considering the circumstances, the giving of information on the matter was defensible, and if he proves that the information was true or that he had reasonable grounds for it, no punishment shall be imposed.

Sec. 2. If the crime mentioned in Section 1 is regarded as grave, a fine or imprisonment for at most two years shall be imposed for *grave defamation.*

In judging the gravity of the crime, special attention shall be paid to whether the information, because of its content or the scope of its dissemination or otherwise, was likely to result in serious damage.

Sec. 3. A person, who vilifies another by an insulting epithet or accusation or by other outrageous conduct toward him, shall be sentenced for *insulting conduct* to pay a fine, if the act is not punishable in accord with Section 1 or 2.

If the crime is grave, a fine or imprisonment for at most six months shall be imposed.

Sec. 4. The defamation of a deceased person shall incur

punishment in accord with Section 1 or 2, if the act is offensive to the survivors or if, considering the time that has passed since the deceased was alive and other circumstances, the act can be regarded as disturbing the peace to which the deceased should be entitled.

Sec. 5. Crimes referred to in Sections 1–3 may not be prosecuted except by the person aggrieved. However, defamation or grave defamation may be prosecuted by the public prosecutor if the person aggrieved reports the crime for prosecution and such prosecution is, for special reasons, found to be called for in the public interest.

If the defamation had been aimed at a deceased person, prosecution may be instituted by the surviving spouse of the deceased, his direct heir, father, mother or siblings, and by the public prosecutor, if prosecution is, for special reasons, found to be called for in the public interest.

If a crime referred to in Sections 1–3 involves an assault against the head of state of a foreign power who is present in Sweden or against a representative of a foreign power in Sweden which is insulting to the foreign power, the crime may be prosecuted by the public prosecutor without regard for the provisions of the first paragraph. However, prosecution may not be instituted without an order from the King or from one authorized by the King. As amended, SFS 1970:225, eff. July 1, 1970 and SFS 1971:874, effective January 1, 1972.

CHAPTER 6

Of Crimes Against Morals

Sec. 1. If a man, by violence upon her or by threat involving imminent danger, forces a woman to have sexual intercourse, he shall be sentenced for *rape* to imprisonment for at least two and at most ten years. Rendering the woman unconscious or otherwise insensible is equivalent to violence.

If in view of the woman's relationship to the man or for some other reason the crime is considered less grave, a sentence to imprisonment for at most four years shall be imposed for *sexual assault.*

Sec. 2. A person who, under circumstances other than those mentioned in Section 1, by unlawful coercion or by gross abuse of that person's dependency makes some one engage in sexual intercourse or other carnal relations, or who practices carnal relations with some one, taking improper advantage of the fact that said person is unconscious or otherwise helpless or is mentally ill or deficient, shall be sentenced for *sexual infringement of liberty* to imprisonment for at most four years.

Sec. 3. If a person has sexual intercourse with a child under fifteen years of age, he shall be sentenced for *carnal abuse of child* to imprisonment for at most four years.

If the offender abused the child outrageously or the crime is otherwise regarded as grave, he shall be sentenced to imprisonment for at least two and at most eight years.

Sec. 4. If a person has sexual relations with some one of the opposite sex who is under eighteen years of age and is in his charge at a school, an institution or some other establishment or is otherwise subject to his supervision, care or authority, or else if it occurs by taking advantage of the minor's dependent situation, he shall be sentenced for *carnal abuse of youth* to imprisonment for at most four years.

The same shall apply if a person who is over eighteen years of age has sexual relations with some one of the same sex who is under eighteen or, under circumstances stated in the first paragraph, with some one of the same sex who is under twenty years of age. As amended, SFS 1969:162, eff. July 1, 1969.

Sec. 5. If a person has sexual relations with his own child or its offspring, he shall be sentenced for *carnal abuse of offspring* to imprisonment for at most two years.

A person who has sexual relations with his sibling shall be sentenced for *carnal abuse of sibling* to imprisonment for at most one year.

The provisions of this Section do not apply to the person who has been made to commit the act by unlawful coercion or other improper means.

Sec. 6. A person, who touches a child under fifteen years of age in a manner violating the sense of decency, shall, unless the act is punishable under prior provisions of this Chapter, be sentenced for *indecent conduct* to pay a fine or to imprisonment for at most one year.

The same shall apply if a person exposes himself to another in a manner apt to give offense or if he otherwise behaves indecently toward him by word or action which flagrantly offends against propriety and morality.

Sec. 7. If a person habitually or for personal gain encourages or exploits another person's immoral mode of life, or if a person entices some one under twenty years of age to enter such a life, he shall be sentenced for *procuring* to imprisonment for at most four years.

If the crime is grave, imprisonment for at least two and at most six years shall be imposed. In judging the gravity of the crime, special attention shall be paid to whether the offender has widely encouraged immoral living or has ruthlessly exploited another.

If a person in order to gain particular profit encourages temporary sexual relations between others, he shall be sentenced for *promoting immorality* to pay a fine or to imprisonment for at most six months. As amended, SFS 1969:162, eff. July 1, 1969.

Sec. 8. A person, who, by promising or giving compensation, obtains or tries to obtain a temporary sexual relationship with some one under eighteen years of age or, if he is of the same sex, under twenty years, shall be sentenced for *seduction of youth* to pay a fine or to imprisonment for at most six months. As amended, SFS 1969:162, eff. July 1, 1969.

Sec. 9. A sanction provided in this Chapter for an act committed against some one under a given age shall be imposed even on a person who did not know but had reasonable grounds for assuming that the other had not reached such age.

Sec. 10. Attempt to commit rape, sexual assault, carnal abuse of child or carnal abuse of youth shall be punished as stated in Chapter 23.

Sec. 11. Rape, sexual assault and attempt to commit these crimes, as well as sexual infringement of liberty may be prosecuted by the public prosecutor only if the person aggrieved reports the crime for prosecution or such prosecution is called for in the public interest.

When six months have passed since the crime was committed, the public prosecutor may not institute prosecution unless a report of the crime had been made before the expiration of that period or it can be shown that a lawful excuse for the failure to report it existed, or prosecution is called for in the public interest. After the expiration of the period mentioned, the person aggrieved may not institute prosecution of the crime, unless it can be shown that a lawful excuse existed.

When, in case of carnal abuse of child, carnal abuse of youth or attempt to commit these crimes, there is little difference in age and development between the offender and the person against whom the crime was committed, public prosecution shall not occur unless it is called for in the public interest.

CHAPTER 7

Of Crimes Against Family

Sec. 1. If a married person enters a new marriage or a single person marries one who is already married, he shall be sentenced for *bigamy* to pay a fine or to imprisonment for at most two years.

Sec. 2. If a person marries one who because of mental illness or temporary mental disorder or for other similar reason is not legally competent to act, or if a person contracts a marriage which upon demand of the other spouse can be annulled on grounds of fraud or deceit, he shall be sentenced for *unlawful marriage* to pay a fine or to imprisonment for at most two years. The same applies when some one forces another into marriage.

Sec. 3. A person, who conceals or exchanges a child or otherwise, by giving incorrect notice to the authorities or by failing to give notice, appropriates for himself or another a false family status or deprives another of his rightful family status, shall be sentenced for *perversion of family status* to pay a fine or to imprisonment for at most two years.

Sec. 4. If a person, without authorization, separates a child under fifteen years of age from the person who has the care of the child, he shall, unless the crime is one against personal liberty, be sentenced for *dealing arbitrarily with a child* to pay a fine or to imprisonment for at most six months.

The same shall apply if a spouse without noteworthy reason arbitrarily takes away a child under fifteen years of age who is placed in charge of both spouses, or if a spouse or other person who is to be in charge of the child without authorization seizes the child and thus takes the law into his own hands.

Sec. 5. Attempt to pervert family status is punished as stated in Chapter 23.

Sec. 6. Unlawful marriage may not be prosecuted unless an annulment of the marriage has been decreed.

Arbitrary dealing with a child may not be prosecuted by the public prosecutor unless prosecution is called for in the public interest.

CHAPTER 8

Of Theft, Robbery and Other Crimes of Stealing

Sec. 1. A person, who, with the intent of appropriating it, unlawfully takes what belongs to another shall, if the appropriation involves loss, be sentenced for *theft* to imprisonment for at most two years.

Sec. 2. If the crime mentioned in Section 1 is regarded as petty, considering the value of the stolen goods and other circumstances of the crime, a sentence to pay a fine or to imprisonment for at most six months shall be imposed for *petty theft.*

Sec. 3. If a person steals from a decedent's estate in which he is part owner, or if spouses, siblings, parents and children, or if foster parents and foster children steal from each other while they live together, a fine or imprisonment for at most one year shall be imposed for *family theft.* If a person steals chattels of which he is a part owner, he too shall be sentenced for the same crime. If several participate in a theft and if what has just been stated applies to any one of them, each of the others shall also be sentenced for family theft except the one who acted with intent to appropriate the stolen goods. As amend, SFS 1971:874 eff. January 1, 1972.

Sec. 4. If the crimes mentioned in Sections 1 and 3 are regarded as grave, imprisonment for at least six months and at most six years shall be imposed for *grand theft.*

In judging the gravity of the crime, special attention shall be paid to whether the crime was committed by breaking and entering or was aimed at an object which someone carried on his person, whether the offender had been equipped with a weapon, explosive or other similar means or whether the act otherwise was of a specially dangerous nature, directed at substantial values or involved a keenly felt loss.

Sec. 5. A person, who steals by means of violence against another or by means of threat implying imminent danger or who, after committing a theft and being caught in the act, resists by such violence or threat the one who wants to recover the stolen property, shall be sentenced for *robbery* to imprisonment for at least one and at most six years. The same shall apply if a person by such violence or threat forces another to do or not do something resulting in gain to the offender and loss to the person so forced or to someone he represents. Rendering a person unconscious or similarly helpless is equivalent to violence.

Sec. 6. If the crime mentioned in Section 5 is regarded as grave, a sentence to imprisonment for at least four and at most ten years shall be imposed for *aggravated robbery.*

In judging the gravity of the crime, special attention shall be paid to whether the violence was dangerous to life or the offender inflicted serious bodily injury or a severe illness or whether he otherwise had shown considerable brutality or had grossly taken advantage of the victim's defenseless or exposed situation.

Sec. 7. If a person unlawfully takes or uses a motor vehicle or other motor-driven conveyance belonging to another, he shall, unless the crime is punishable under earlier provisions of this Chapter, be sentenced for *vehicle theft* to imprisonment for at most two years or, if the crime is of a petty nature, to pay a fine.

If the crime is grave, imprisonment for at least six months and at most four years shall be imposed.

Sec. 8. A person, who, in a case other than those specially mentioned in this Chapter, unlawfully takes and uses or otherwise appropriates something, shall be sentenced for *arbitrary conduct* to pay a fine or to imprisonment for at most six months. The same shall apply, if a person, without appropriating anything, by affixing or breaking a lock or by other means unlawfully trespasses on another's possession or by violence or threat of violence prevents another from exercising his right to retain or take something.

If the crime is grave, imprisonment for at most two years shall be imposed.

Sec. 9. If a person unlawfully trespasses on another's possession in order to take the law into his own hands, he shall be sentenced for *self-help* to pay a fine or to imprisonment for at most six months.

Sec. 10. If a person unlawfully diverts electric energy, he shall be sentenced for *unlawful diversion of energy* to pay a fine or to imprisonment for at most two years.

Sec. 11. If a person unlawfully takes from forest of field such objects as are mentioned in Chapter 12, Section 2, second paragraph, and if the crime is not to be considered as trespass as there described the provisions of the present Chapter with reference to theft shall apply.

If a person trespasses on another's possession of real property, for instance by unlawfully raising or breaking down a fence, or by building, digging, plowing, making a road or letting cattle graze, or if a person without authorization deprives another of possessing real property or a part thereof, the provisions in Sections 8 and 9 with respect to arbitrary conduct and self-help shall apply.

Sec. 12. Attempt or preparation to commit theft, grand theft, robbery, aggravated robbery, vehicle theft or unlawful diversion of energy, as well as conspiracy to commit or failure to reveal robbery or aggravated robbery shall be punished as stated in Chapter 23. If a completed vehicle theft should have been regarded as petty, no such punishment shall be imposed, however.

Sec. 13. If a crime referred to in this Chapter, other than grand theft, robbery or aggravated robbery, has been committed against the spouse or the betrothed of the offender or of another accessory to the crime, or against sibling, a blood relation in ascending or descending line or one equally closely related by marriage, or against foster parents or foster children, the public prosecutor may institute prosecution only if the person aggrieved has reported the crime for prosecution or such prosecution is called for in the public interest.

In applying the provisions just stated, receiving stolen goods and petty receiving of stolen goods shall also be regarded as accessory. As amend, SFS 1971:874, eff. January 1, 1972.

CHAPTER 9

Of Fraud and Other Dishonesty

Sec. 1. A person, who by deception induces some one to do or not to do something which involves gain for the offender and loss for the dupe or some one he represents, shall be sentenced for *fraud* to imprisonment for at most two years.

Sec. 2. If, considering the size of the loss and other circumstances of the crime mentioned in Section 1, the offense is regarded as petty, a fine or imprisonment for at most six months shall be imposed for *fraudulent conduct.*

If a person uses lodging, meals, transportation or admission to a show or something similar offered on condition of payment in cash, and he fails to meet his obligation, he shall, whether he deceived any one or not, be sentenced for fradulent conduct or, if the crime is not regarded as petty, for fraud. The same shall apply if a person, who has to serve the public at a fixed rate, takes payment in excess of that rate without indicating the discrepancy.

Sec. 3. If a crime referred to earlier in this Chapter is regarded as grave, imprisonment for at least six months and at most six years shall be imposed for *gross fraud.*

In judging the gravity of the crime, special attention shall be paid to whether the offender had abused public trust or employed a false document or misleading bookkeeping, or the crime otherwise had been of a particularly dangerous nature, had involved a substantial value or had resulted in a keenly felt loss.

Sec. 4. A person, who by unlawful coercion induces some one to do or not do something which involves gain for the offender and loss for the coerced person or someone he represents, shall, unless the crime is regarded as robbery or aggravated robbery, be sentenced for *extortion* to imprisonment for at most two years or, if the crime is petty, to pay a fine.

If the crime is grave, imprisonment for at least six months and at most six years shall be imposed.

Sec. 5. A person who in connection with a contract or some other legal transaction takes advantage of some one's distress, ignorance, foolishness or dependent relationship to him, in order to obtain a benefit which is clearly disproportionate to the compensation or for which no compensation will be made, shall be sentenced for *usury* to pay a fine or to imprisonment for at most two years.

If the crime is grave, imprisonment for at least six months and at most four years shall be imposed.

Sec. 6. A person, who buys something of which another has been dispossessed by crime or utilizes it or otherwise deals with it so as to render its restitution difficult, shall be sentenced for *receiving stolen goods* to imprisonment for at most two years or, if the crime was petty, to pay a fine or to imprisonment for at most six months. The same shall apply if some one procures undue gain from another's criminal proceeds, and also if a person by dunning, assignment or in other like manner asserts a claim arisen from a crime.

If the crime is grave, imprisonment for at least six months and at most four years shall be imposed.

Sec. 7. If the offender in a case referred to in Section 6 was unaware of but had reasonable grounds for assuming that a crime was involved, he shall be sentenced for *petty receiving of stolen goods* to pay a fine or to imprisonment for at most six months.

A person shall also be sentenced for petty receiving of stolen goods if he, in a manner stated in Section 6, was an accessory to the crime which dispossessed another of his property and while unaware of it had reasonable grounds for assuming that a crime was being committed.

Sec. 8. A person, who, in a case other than those referred to earlier in this Chapter, acts dishonestly in that he, by misleading some one induces him to do or not to do something and thereby harms him or some one he represents, shall be sentenced for *dishonest conduct* to pay a fine or to imprisonment for at most two years. As amended, SFS 1970:414, eff. Jan. 1, 1971.

Sec. 9. A person, who publishes or otherwise distributes among people misleading information in order to influence the price of an article, a paper of value or other property, shall be sentenced for *swindle* to imprisonment for at most two years, or, if the crime is petty, to pay a fine.

If a person who assists in organizing a joint-stock company or other enterprise or who because of his position ought to posses special knowledge about an enterprise, intentionally or due to gross carelessness publishes or otherwise spreads among people generally or those interested in the enterprise misleading information apt to influence the evaluation of the enterprise from an economic point of view and thereby causes a loss, shall be sentenced as stated in the first paragraph.

If a crime referred to in this Section is regarded as grave, imprisonment for at least six months and at most four years shall be imposed.

Sec. 10. If a person accepts, for use as a means of exerting pressure in connection with a claim, a document that is false, drawn for the sake of appearance or otherwise incorrect, or else a check drawn on insufficient funds, he shall be sentenced for *usurious acquisition* to pay a fine or to imprisonment for at most two years.

Sec. 11. Attempt or preparation to commit fraud, gross fraud, extortion or usury shall be punished as stated in Chapter 23; however, what is stated in Chapter 23, Section 3, shall not apply in the case of attempt at extortion.

A person, who in order to defraud an insurer or otherwise with fraudulent intent inflicts bodily harm on himself or another or harm to property of his own or of another, shall be sentenced as for preparation to commit fraud or gross fraud. The same shall apply if a person with the intent just mentioned attempts to bring about such harm. If before the harm has been done, he has voluntarily refrained from carrying out the act, he shall be absolved of punishment.

Sec. 12. What is stated in Chapter 8, Section 13, concerning restriction of a public prosecutor's right to prosecute shall have corresponding application to crimes referred to in the present Chapter, except for gross fraud.

CHAPTER 10

Of Embezzlement and Other Breaches of Trust

Sec. 1. If a person, who, owing to a contract or to public or private service or a similar situation, has gained possession of property on behalf of another and with the obligation to deliver it or account for it, by appropriating the property or otherwise disregarding what he has to comply with in order to be able to fulfill his duty, he shall, if the act results in gain for him and loss to the owner, be sentenced for *embezzlement* to imprisonment for at most two years.

Sec. 2. If the crime referred to in Section 1 is regarded as petty, considering the value of the property and other circumstances, a fine or imprisonment for at most six months shall be imposed for *withholding property.*

Sec. 3. If the crime referred to in Section 1 is regarded as grave, imprisonment for at least six months and at most six years shall be imposed for *gross embezzlement.*

In judging the gravity of the crime, special attention shall be paid to whether the offender had abused a responsible position or used a false document or misleading bookkeeping or whether the act otherwise had been of a specially dangerous nature, had involved a substantial amount or had resulted in a keenly felt loss.

Sec. 4. A person, who, in a case other than one heretofore mentioned in this Chapter, takes any step with regard to property in his possession to which the right of ownership or protection is reserved for, guaranteed to or otherwise belongs to another and the latter is by such step dispossessed of his property or otherwise deprived of his right, shall be sentenced for *unlawful disposal* to pay a fine or to imprisonment for at most two years.

Sec. 5. If a person, who, on account of his position of trust, whether in public or in private service, as manager or otherwise, has been given the task of handling another's economic affair or to exercise supervision over its management, misuses his authority to represent his principal or misuses his position of trust and thereby causes a loss to his principal, he shall, if the crime is not punishable under Sections 1–3, be sentenced for *disloyalty to principal* to pay a fine or to imprisonment for at most two years.

If the crime is grave, imprisonment for at least six months and at most six years shall be imposed. In judging the gravity of the crime, special attention shall be paid to whether the offender had used a false document or misleading bookkeeping or had caused his principal a substantial or keenly felt loss.

If a person, who has been given the handling of another's legal affair, misuses his position of trust to the disadvantage of his prinicpal, he shall be sentenced as stated in Section 1 even though the affair is not of an economic nature.

Sec. 6. A person, who, in a case not heretofore mentioned in this Chapter, by misusing his authority to take a legal action on behalf of another, harms that person or by misuse of his authority to call a promissory note or like instrument lays claim to something that belongs to another, shall be sentenced for *misuse of authority* to pay a fine or to imprisonment for at most two years. The same shall apply if a person demands payment in conformity with a document that has not been issued or of a debt already liquidated or demands the delivery of goods he has already received or, when dunned, alleges a receipt which has not been given.

Sec. 7. If a person unlawfully uses something in his possession which belongs to another and thereby causes loss or inconvenience, he shall be sentenced for *unlawful use* to pay a fine or to imprisonment for at most six months. The same shall apply if the occupant of real estate uses it to the detriment of another's right to it, by unlawfully building, digging, plowing, making roads, letting cattle graze, or other like action.

Sec. 8. If a person does not comply with the law's requirement concerning the obligation to give notice of found property or of something belonging to another, of which he has gained possession by error or by chance, he shall be sentenced for *failure to return lost property* to pay a fine. If he disregards such obligation with the intent to appropriate the property or otherwise deals with the property in a manner mentioned in Section 4, the provisions of that Section shall apply.

Sec. 9. Attempt at embezzlement, gross embezzlement or disloyalty to principal shall be punished as stated in Chapter 23.

Sec. 10. What is stated in Chapter 8 Section 13, concerning restriction of a public prosecutor's right to prosecute shall have corresponding application to crimes referred to in this Chapter, except gross embezzlement and disloyalty to principal which is considered grave.

Unlawful disposal of property, which has come into the offender's possession through a contract according to which the property right shall be transferred only after full payment has been made, may not be prosecuted by the public prosecutor unless for special reason such prosecution is called for in the public interest.

CHAPTER 11

Of Crimes in Connection with Debts

Sec. 1. A debtor, who destroys or by gift or other like action dispossesses himself of substantial property and thereby reduces himself to insolvency or aggravates his insolvent condition, shall be sentenced for *dishonesty to creditors* to imprisonment for at most two years.

A debtor, who, in connection with bankruptcy or official negotiation with creditors short of bankruptcy, or in an inventory sworn to in a distraint proceeding, conceals an asset, reports a nonexistent debt, or gives other erroneous information of like nature, shall also, unless the statement is corrected before it is attested by oath or otherwise made the basis of the proceeding, be sentenced for dishonesty to creditors. The same shall apply if a debtor, in connection with some other executory proceeding invokes an erroneous document or a fictitious contract and thereby prevents the seizure, through the proceeding, of property adequate to provide a creditor with payment or protection.

A debtor, who, when bankruptcy is impending, removes an important asset from the Realm with intent to withhold it from the bankruptcy, as well as a debtor, who in a bankruptcy withdraws or withholds an asset from the receiver, shall likewise be sentenced for dishonesty to creditors.

Sec. 2. If the crime referred to in Sec. 1 is considered grave, imprisonment for at least six months and at most six years shall be imposed for *gross dishonesty to creditors.*

In judging the gravity of the crime, special attention shall be paid to whether the debtor had sworn to the truth of an erroneous statement or had used a false document or misleading bookkeeping or whether the crime had been one of large scale.

Sec. 3. A debtor, who continues to operate a business, expending considerable sums without corresponding profit to the business, or lives extravagantly or gets involved in a risky enterprise or a foolish assumption of liability or takes some like step, thereby intentionally or through gross carelessness causing or aggravating his insolvency, shall be sentenced for *careless disregard of creditors* to imprisonment for at most two years.

A debtor, who in connection with bankruptcy or an official negotiation with creditors short of bankruptcy or in an inventory sworn to in a distraint proceeding, due to gross carelessness conceals an asset, reports a non-existent debt or gives some other erroneous statement of like nature, shall also, unless the statement is corrected before it is attested by oath or otherwise made the basis of the proceeding, be sentenced for careless disregard of creditors.

Sec. 4. A debtor, who, when bankruptcy is impending, pays a creditor's claim or furnishes security therefor or takes some other like step and thereby considerably encroaches upon the rights of the rest of the creditors, shall be sentenced for *favoritism to creditor* to imprisonment for at most two years. The same shall apply, if a debtor, who is under obligation to keep accounts, acts in the manner here stated although he obviously should, in accord with good business customs, have suspended payments.

A debtor, who, for the purpose of furthering an agreement, secretly makes or promises payment or other advantage, shall also be sentenced for favoritism to creditor.

Sec. 5. If a debtor intentionally or through carelessness so disregards the duty incumbent on him to keep accounts that the condition and the trend of the enterprise cannot on the whole be judged with the aid of the account books, he shall be sentenced for *bookkeeping crime* to imprisonment for at most two years or, if the crime is petty, to pay a fine.

Prosecution for bookkeeping crime may take place only if the debtor, within five years from the time the crime was committed, has become bankrupt, has received or offered an agreement, or has suspended payments.

Sec. 6. Attempt to remove an asset from the Realm, as mentioned in Section 1, third paragraph, shall be punished as stated in Chapter 23.

Sec. 7. If a person representing a debtor commits a crime mentioned in this Chapter, he shall be punished as though he himself were a debtor.

A creditor, who, in a case described in Section 4, accepts or lets himself be promised payment, security or other advantage, shall be punished as an accessory to the crime only if he employs undue threats or undue promise of a favor or acts on the basis of a secret understanding with the debtor.

CHAPTER 12

Of Crimes Inflicting Damage

Sec. 1. A person, who destroys or damages real property or chattels to the detriment of another's right thereto, shall be sentenced for *inflicting damage* to pay a fine or to imprisonment for at most six months.

Sec. 2. If, considering the minimal harm and other circumstances of the act, the crime mentioned in Section 1 is regarded as petty, a fine shall be imposed for *trespass*.

A person, who in forest or field unlawfully takes growing trees or grass or from growing trees takes twigs, branches, birch bark, bark, leaves, bast, acorns, nuts or resin, or takes fallen trees, stone, gravel, sod or similar things not prepared for use, shall be sentenced for trespass if the crime is regarded as petty considering the value of what is taken and other circumstance.

Sec. 3. If the crime referred to in Section 1 is regarded as grave, imprisonment for at most four years shall be imposed for *inflicting gross damage.*

In judging the gravity of the crime, special attention shall be paid to whether the act had given rise to a substantial danger to some one's life or health or damage had been done to something of great cultural or economic importance or else is keenly felt.

Sec. 4. If a person unlawfully takes his way across a building lot, a plantation or other land that can be damaged thereby, he shall be sentenced for *taking unlawful path* to pay a fine.

Sec. 5. Attempt or preparation to inflict gross damage and failure to reveal such crime shall be punished as stated in Chapter 23.

Sec. 6. Trespass or taking unlawful path may, if the crime only infringes the right of a private person, be subject to public prosecution only if, for special reasons, such prosecution is called for in the public interest.

CHAPTER 13

Of Crimes Involving Public Danger

Sec. 1. If a person starts a fire that imports danger to another's life or health or extensive destruction of another's property, he shall be sentenced for *arson* to imprisonment for at least two and at most eight years.

Sec. 2. If the crime mentioned in Section 1 is considered grave, imprisonment for a fixed term of at least six and at most ten years, or for life, shall be imposed for *grave arson.*

In judging the gravity of the crime, special attention shall be paid to whether the fire was set in a thickly populated area, where it could easily spread, or had otherwise threatened danger to several persons or to property of special importance.

Sec. 3. A person, who causes an explosion, inundation, landslide, shipwreck, airplane or train accident or other like calamity and thereby gives rise to a danger to another's life or health or of extensive destruction of another's property, shall be sentenced for *devastation endangering the public* to imprisonment for at least two and at most eight years.

If the crime is grave, imprisonment for a fixed term of at least six and at most ten years, or for life, shall be imposed.

Sec. 4. If a person destroys or damages property of significant importance for the defense of the Realm, public subsistence, judicial or public administration, or the maintenance of public order and security in the Realm, or by some other action, not limited to the withholding of manpower or advocacy to that effect, seriously distrubs or interferes with the use of such property, he shall be sentenced for *sabotage* to imprisonment for at most four years. The same shall apply, if a person otherwise, by inflicting damage or by other action just mentioned, seriously disturbs or interferes with public traffic or the use of telegraph, telephone, radio or other like public service or some installation that supplies the public with water, light, heat, or power.

Sec. 5. If a crime mentioned in Section 4 is considered grave, imprisonment for a fixed term of at least two and at most ten years, or for life, shall be imposed for *gross sabotage.*

In judging the gravity of the crime, special attention shall be paid to whether it produced danger to the security of the Realm, to the lives of several persons, or to property of special importance.

Sec. 5a. A person on board an aircraft who by means of unlawful force seizes the aircraft or interferes with its operation shall be sentenced for *aircraft hijacking* to imprisonment for at most four years.

If the crime is grave, imprisonment for at least one and at most ten years shall be imposed. In judging the gravity of the crime, special attention shall be paid to whether it produced danger to the lives of others or if the offense was otherwise of a specially dangerous type. Added, SFS 1971:188, eff. June 9, 1971.

Sec. 6. A person, who carelessly, by the careless handling of fire or explosive or otherwise, causes a fire or some calamity mentioned in Section 1, 2, or 3 or a danger of its occurring, or causes damage or interference referred to in Section 4, shall be sentenced for *carelessness endangering the public* to pay a fine or to imprisonment for at most six months.

If the crime is grave, imprisonment for at most two years shall be imposed.

Sec. 7. If a person creates a general danger to peoples' life or health by poisoning or infecting food, water, or the like, or in other ways by spreading poison or such, or by transmitting or spreading serious disease, he shall be sentenced for *spreading poison or contagion* to imprisonment for at most six years.

If the crime is grave, imprisonment for a fixed term of at least four and at most ten years, or for life, shall be imposed. In judging the gravity of the crime, special attention shall be paid to whether it was committed with intent to harm another's life or health or whether it exposed many persons to danger.

Sec. 8. If a person creates a general danger to animals or plants by means of poison or by transmitting or spreading virulent disease or by spreading pernicious animals or weeds or by other like means, he shall be sentenced for *destruction* to pay a fine or to imprisonment for at most two years.

If the crime is grave, imprisonment for at least six months and at most six years shall be imposed. In judging the gravity of the crime, special attention shall be paid to whether it was committed with intent to harm or whether property of substantial value was exposed to danger.

Sec. 9. If a person acts as stated in Section 7 or 8 due to gross carelessness, he shall be sentenced for *careless handling of poison or contagion* to pay a fine or to imprisonment for at most two years.

Sec. 10. If a person, without incurring liability to punishment in accord with preceding provisions of this Chapter, while handling fire, explosive or poison or in some other way creates a danger of fire or calamity referred to in Section 1, 2, or 3 or of general danger referred to in Section 7 or 8, and neglects, when having become aware of the danger, to do all that can be reasonably expected of him to avert it, he shall be sentenced for *neglect to avert public danger* to pay a fine or to imprisonment for at most one year.

Sec. 11. If a person, who has become liable to punishment in accord with Section 1, 2, 3, 6, 7, 8, 9, or 10, has voluntarily averted the danger there mentioned before any considerable harm developed, he may be sentenced to a lesser punishment than that provided for the crime; however, no lesser punishment than imprisonment may be imposed, if the minimum sanction for the crime is otherwise imprisonment for two years or longer. If the danger was minor and the act is not punishable by more than a year's imprisonment, no punishment shall be imposed.

Sec. 12. Attempt, preparation or conspiracy to commit arson, gross arson, devastation endangering the public, sabotage, gross sabotage, aircraft hi-jacking, spreading poison or contagion, or destruction, as well as neglect to avert such a crime shall be punished as stated in Chapter 23. As amended, SFS 1971:188, eff. June 9, 1971.

CHAPTER 14

Of Crimes of Falsification

Sec. 1. A person, who, by writing the name of another person, real or fictitious, or by deceit obtains another's signature or in other ways produces a false document, or who deceitfully alters or adds to a genuine document, shall, if the act jeopardizes proof, be sentenced for *document forgery* to imprisonment for at most two years.

By document is meant a protocol, contract, promissory note, certificate or other record prepared to serve as evidence or otherwise important as evidence; also an identification card, ticket or similar evidential token.

Sec. 2. If the crime mentioned in Section 1 is regarded as petty a sentence to pay a fine or to imprisonment for at most six months shall be imposed for *tampering with document.*

In judging the pettiness of the crime, special attention shall be paid to whether the document was of little importance such as a cash receipt, counter token or like proof of receipt, or the act was committed to aid another to gain his right.

Sec. 3. If the crime referred to in Section 1 is considered grave, imprisonment for at least six months and at most six years shall be imposed for *gross document forgery.*

In judging the gravity of the crime, special attention shall be paid to whether the forgery involved some authority's archival document of great importance or a document of special importance in general commerce such as a bond, a share certificate or a mortgage or whether the act was in other ways of a particularly harmful kind.

Sec. 4. A person, who destroys, renders unserviceable or secretes a document, which he has no right at the time to dispose of in such manner, shall, if the act jeopardizes proof, be sentenced for *suppression of document* to imprisonment for at most two years or, if the crime is petty to pay a fine or to imprisonment for at most six months.

If the crime is grave, imprisonment for at least six months and at most four years shall be imposed.

Sec. 5. If some one without permission affixes to or otherwise forges another person's name or signature on a creation of applied art or on some other such product and thereby makes it appear that such person has proved himself to be the originator of the product, he shall be sentenced for *forgery of signature* to imprisonment for at most two years or, if the crime is petty, to pay a fine or to imprisonment for at most six months.

If the crime is grave, imprisonment for at least six months and at most four years shall be imposed. As amended, SFS 1970:489, eff. October 1, 1970.

Sec. 6. A person, who counterfeits a banknote or coin valid within or outside the Realm or otherwise forges a note or a coin, shall be sentenced for *counterfeiting currency* to imprisonment for at most four years or, if the crime is petty, to pay a fine or to imprisonment for at most six months.

If the crime is grave, imprisonment for at least two and at most eight years shall be imposed.

Sec. 7. If a person, who counterfeits a valid postage stamp, cover stamp or other domestic or foreign stamp indicating value, whether official or meant for general use, or an official domestic or foreign control stamp on a measure, weight, merchandise, document or other thing, or falsely affixes such stamp or, deceitfully, a genuine stamp, or if he forges such a stamp or the object stamped, he shall, if the act jeopardizes proof, be sentenced for *stamp forgery* to imprisonment for at most two years or, if the crime is petty, to pay a fine or to imprisonment for at most six months.

If the crime is grave, imprisonment for at least six months and at most four years shall be imposed.

Sec. 8. If a person deceitfully places a mark or other object which can be taken to be a valid boundary mark, water mark, fixed point or other mark for the measure of surface or height, or if he moves, takes away, injures or destroys such a mark, he shall, if the act jeopardizes proof, be sentenced for *falsification of fixed mark* to imprisonment for at most four years or, if the crime is petty, to pay a fine or to imprisonment for at most six months.

Sec. 9. A person, who invokes a false document, offers or holds for sale a work with a false signature, utters counterfeit currency, uses a false mark indicating value or a false control stamp, invokes a false fixed mark or otherwise makes use of anything that has been falsified in a manner stated above, shall, if the act jeopardizes proof, be sentenced for the use of what was falsified as if he himself had done the falsification.

Sec. 10. A person, who, in a case other than those referred to in Section 9, distributes among people something that can easily be mistaken for a valid banknote, coin or other official token of value, shall be sentenced for *illegal distribution of imitations* to pay a fine.

Sec. 11. If a person, who has incurred liability to punishment according to earlier provisions of this Chapter, voluntarily and before any considerable inconvenience has arisen, has averted the danger from the point of view of proof that the act imported, he may be sentenced to a lesser punishment than the one provided for the crime. If the danger was minimal and no more serious punishment was provided for the act than imprisonment for six months, no punishment shall be imposed.

Sec. 12. Attempt or preparation to commit document forgery, gross document forgery, suppression of document, forgery of signature, counterfeiting of currency, stamp forgery, falsification of fixed mark, or using something which is falsified, as well as failure to disclose the counterfeiting of currency, shall be punished as stated in Chapter 23. If the crime would have been regarded as petty, had it been completed, such punishment shall not be imposed.

CHAPTER 15

Of Perjury, False Prosecution, and Other Untrue Statements

Sec. 1. If a person, under legal oath or affirmation instead of oath, gives untrue information or withholds the truth, he shall be sentenced for *perjury* to imprisonment for at most four years or, if the crime is petty, to pay a fine or to imprisonment for at most six months.

If the crime is grave, imprisonment for at least two and at most eight years shall be imposed. In judging the gravity of the crime, special attention shall be paid to whether it was done with the intent that an innocent person be punished for a grave crime or that very considerable harm be inflicted upon some one.

Sec. 2. A person, who, during a hearing in a judicial proceeding, after declaring that he will tell the truth gives untrue information or withholds the truth, shall be sentenced for *untrue statement by a party* to imprisonment for at most two years or, if the crime is petty, to pay a fine or to imprisonment for at most six months.

Sec. 3. If a person commits an act, referred to in Section 1 or 2, due to gross carelessness, he shall be sentenced for *careless statement* to pay a fine or to imprisonment for at most six months.

Sec. 4. If a statement referred to in Sections 1–3 is proved to be without significance for the issue, no punishment shall be imposed.

What has just been said shall also apply if a person has given untrue information or has withheld the truth with regard to something about which he would have had the right to refuse to express himself and the circumstances furnish him with a reasonable excuse.

Sec. 5. If some one institutes the prosecution of an innocent person with the intent that such person be convicted, he shall be sentenced for *false prosecution* to imprisonment for at most two years or, if the crime was petty, to pay a fine or to imprisonment for at most six months.

If the crime is grave, imprisonment for at least six months and at most four years shall be imposed. In judging the gravity of the crime, special attention shall be paid to whether the prosecution had concerned a serious crime or had involved misuse of an official position.

A person who institutes prosecution although he lacks probable cause for so doing shall be sentenced for *unjustified prosecution* to pay a fine or to imprisonment for at most six months.

Sec. 6. If some one denounces an innocent person for prosecution with the intent that such person be convicted, he shall be sentenced for *false accusation* to imprisonment for at most two years or, if the crime is petty, to pay a fine or to imprisonment for at most six months.

If he did not realize but had reasonable grounds for assuming that the accused was innocent, he shall be sentenced for *unjustified accusation* to pay a fine or to imprisonment for at most six months.

Sec. 7. A person, who, in a case other than those referred to in Section 6, before a prosecutor, police authority or other authority untruthfully charges another with a criminal act, alleges some compromising circumstances, or denies an exonerating or extenuating circumstance, shall, if the authority has to receive reports of this kind, be sentenced for *false incrimination* to imprisonment for at most two years or, if the crime is petty, to pay a fine or to imprisonment for at most six months.

If he did not realize but had reasonable grounds for assuming that the information was untrue, he shall be sentenced for *careless incrimination* to pay a fine or to imprisonment for at most six months.

Sec. 8. If a person tampers with or removes evidence with the intent that an innocent person be convicted, or if he with such intent invokes false evidence, he shall be sentenced for *tampering with evidence* to imprisonment for at most two years or, if the crime is petty, to pay a fine or to imprisonment for at most six months.

If the crime is grave, imprisonment for at least six months

and at most four years shall be imposed.

Sec. 9. If a person not liable to punishment in accord with previous provisions in this Chapter has by any act there mentioned given rise to a danger that some one be, without legal cause, convicted or otherwise suffer considerable harm, and if once having realized this, he neglects to do what reasonably can be asked of him to avert the harm, he shall be sentenced for *neglect to avert judicial error* to pay a fine or to imprisonment for at most six months.

Sec. 10. If, in a written deposition which according to law or statute is made under oath or on one's faith and honor or like affirmation, a person gives untrue information or withholds the truth, he shall, if the act jeopardizes proof, be sentenced for *untrue affirmation* to pay a fine or to imprisonment for at most six months or, if the crime is grave, to imprisonment for at most two years.

If such action is due to gross carelessness, a sentence to pay a fine or to imprisonment for at most six months shall be imposed for *careless affirmation.*

Sec. 11. If, in a certificate or other document, a person gives untrue information about his identity or about other than his own concerns, or if a person for the sake of appearances prepares a document concerning judicial act, he shall, if the action jeopardizes proof, be sentenced for *false certification* to pay a fine or to imprisonment for at most six months. If the crime is considered grave because it involves misuse of official position or for other reasons, imprisonment for at most two years shall be imposed.

A person, who invokes or otherwise uses a false document referred to in the first paragraph, shall, if the act jeopardizes proof, be sentenced, as there provided, for *using a false document.*

Sec. 12. If a person misuses a passport, testimonial or similar document issued in the name of a given individual, by representing himself or another as being that individual or gives out the document to be thus misused, or if he falsely represents a a document, which is a carbon copy or produced by photography or otherwise, as being a correct copy of a given document, he shall, if the act jeopardizes proof, be sentenced for *misuse of document* to pay a fine or to imprisonment for at most six months or, if the crime is grave, to imprisonment for at most two years.

Sec. 13. If a person denies his signature on a document, he shall, if the act jeopardizes proof, be sentenced for *denial of signature* to pay a fine or to imprisonment for at most six months or, if the crime is grave, to imprisonment for at most two years.

Sec. 14. If a person liable to punishment in accord with previous provisions of this Chapter, voluntarily and before a considerable inconvenience has arisen, has corrected the mistake or in other manner averted the risk of further inconvenience, he may be sentenced to a lesser punishment than is provided for the act. If the risk was minimal and the act is not punishable by more than six months' imprisonment, no punishment shall be imposed.

Sec. 15. Preparation to commit perjury or conspiracy to commit perjury which signifies that some one is trying to instigate that act, as well as attempt to tamper with evidence shall be punished as stated in Chapter 23. If the crime would have been regarded as petty, had it been completed, no punishment as just mentioned shall be imposed.

CHAPTER 16

Of Crimes Against Public Order

Sec. 1. If a crowd of people disturbs public order by demonstrating an intention to use group violence in opposition to a public authority or otherwise to compel or obstruct a given measure and does not disperse when ordered to do so by the authority, instigators and leaders shall be sentenced to imprisonment for at most four years and other participants in the crowd's business to pay a fine or to imprisonment for at most two years for *riot*.

If the crowd disperses on order of the authority, instigators and leaders shall be sentenced for riot to pay a fine or to imprisonment for at most two years.

Sec. 2. If a crowd, with intent referred to in Sec. 1., has

proceeded to use group violence on person or property, whether a public authority was present or not, sentences for *violent riot* shall be imposed; on instigators and leaders to imprisonment for at most ten years and on participants in the crowd's business to pay a fine or to imprisonment for at most four years.

Sec. 3. If a member of a crowd that disturbs public order neglects to obey a command aimed at maintaining order, or if he intrudes on an area that is protected or has been closed off against intrusion, he shall, if no riot is occurring, be sentenced for *disobeying police order* to pay a fine or to imprisonment for at most six months.

Sec. 4. If a person by act of violence, loud noise or other like means disturbs or tries to interfere with a public religious service, other public devotional excercise, wedding, funeral or like ceremony, a court session or other state or local official function, or a public gathering for deliberation, instruction or hearing a lecture, he shall be sentenced for *disturbing a function or public meeting* to pay a fine or to imprisonment for at most six months.

Sec. 5. A person, who orally, before a crowd or congregation of people, or in a publication distributed or issued for distribution, or in other message to the public, urges or otherwise attempts to entice people to commit a criminal act, evade a civic duty or disobey public authority, shall be sentenced for *inciting rebellion* to pay a fine or to imprisonment for at most six months.

If the crime is considered grave because the offender tried to induce the commission of a serious crime or for other reasons, imprisonment for at most four years shall be imposed. No responsibility shall be imposed where the crime is petty. In deciding whether the crime should be considered petty, special consideration shall be given to whether there was only insignificant danger that the urging or the attempt might be followed. As amended, SFS 1970:225, eff. July 1, 1970.

Sec. 6. If a person publicly spreads a false rumor or other untrue assertion apt to arouse a danger to public subsistence or to public order or security, he shall be sentenced for *spreading socially harmful rumor* to pay a fine or to imprisonment for at most two years.

Sec. 7. Repealed, SFS 1970:225, eff. February 17, 1971 (SFS 1971:29)

Sec. 8. If a person publicly or otherwise in a statement or other communication which is spread among the public threatens or expresses contempt for a group of a certain race, skin color, national or ethnic origin or religious creed, he shall be sentenced for *agitation against ethnic group* to imprisonment for at most two years or, if the crime is petty, to pay a fine. As amended, SFS 1970:224, eff. Feb. 17, 1971 (SFS:29).

Sec. 9. If a businessman in the conduct of his business discriminates against someone on the ground of his race, skin color, national or ethnic origin or religious creed by refusing to deal with him on the same conditions the businessman applies to others in the conduct of his business, he shall be sentenced to *unlawful discrimination* to pay a fine or to imprisonment for at most six months.

The provisions in the first paragraph concerning businessmen shall be applied correspondingly to a person who is employed in a business or who acts in behalf of a businessman as well as to a person who has a position as a civil servant in which he has to deal with the public.

An organizer of a public assembly or entertainment or an assistant to such organizer may be sentenced for *unlawful discrimination* if he discriminates against someone on the ground of his race, skin color, national or ethnic origin, or religious creed by refusing to allow him to enter the assembly or entertainment on the same conditions which apply to others. Repealed, SFS 1970:225 and a new section, earlier named 16:8a, added SFS 1970:224 and 225, eff. February 17, 1971 (SFS 1971:29).

Sec. 10. If a person, without authorization, moves, or if he injures or infamously treats the corpse or ashes of the dead, opens a grave or otherwise inflicts damage on or abuses a coffin, urn, grave or other resting place of the dead or a tombstone, he shall be sentenced for *crime against the peace of the tomb* to pay a fine or to imprisonment for at most six months.

Sec. 11. If a person, on or at a public place, exhibits pornographic pictures by means of displays or other similar procedure in a manner which is likely to result in public offense, he shall be sentenced for *unlawful exposition of pornographic pictures* to pay a fine or to imprisonment for at most six months. The same applies to a person who sends through the mail to or otherwise furnishes another with pornographic pictures without previous request. As amended, SFS 1970:225, eff. February 17, 1971 (SFS 1971:29).

Sec. 12. A person, who distributes among children or youth a writing or picture which due to its content can coarsen or otherwise involve serious risk for the moral nurture of the young, shall be sentenced for *leading youth astray* to pay a fine or to imprisonment for at most six months.

Sec. 13. If a person, by physical maltreatment, overworking, neglect or in other ways unjustifiably exposes an animal to suffering, he shall be sentenced for *cruelty to animal* to pay a fine or to imprisonment for at most two years. As amended, SFS 1965:726, eff. July 1, 1966.

Sec. 14. If a person organizes for the public a game of chance about money or monetary values, or permits such play on premises he has opened to the public, he shall be sentenced for *gambling* to pay a fine or to imprisonment for at most six months. If a person participates in such play, which has been arranged for the public or else occurs on premises to which the public is admitted, he shall be sentenced for gambling to pay a fine.

Sec. 15. A person, who, in a public place, indoors or outdoors, appears so intoxicated by alcoholic beverages that it is evident from his gestures and speech, shall be sentenced for *drunkenness* to pay a fine of at most five hundred kronor.

The fine just mentioned shall also be imposed if the intoxication has been caused by something other than alcoholic beverages.

Sec. 16. A person, who, in a case other than those previously mentioned in this Chapter, by loud noisiness in a public place or otherwise publicly behaves in a manner apt to arouse public indignation, shall be sentenced for *disorderly conduct* to pay a fine of at most five hundred kronor.

CHAPTER 17

Of Crimes Against Public Activity

Sec. 1. If a person, by violence or threat of violence, attacks a civil servant or some one holding another public office carrying official responsibility while such official is exercising his public function, or does so to compel him to perform or to prevent him from performing an official act, or for the purpose of taking revenge for such act, he shall be sentenced for *violence or threat to public servant* to imprisonment for at most four years or, if the crime is petty, to pay a fine or to imprisonment for at most six months. The same shall apply, if a person attacks some one who has been a civil servant or has held other office carrying official responsibility, for something he had done or failed to do while in office.

The statement just made concerning a position carrying official responsibility shall also apply to a position which enjoys the same protection in accord with the King's decree.

Sec. 2. If a person, who, otherwise than stated in Section 1, in order to compel or prevent some one who enjoys the protection referred to in said Section from exercising his duties or in order to take revenge for an official act, wrongfully engages in an act which causes such person suffering, injury or inconvenience, or threatens such consequence, he shall be sentenced for *outrageous conduct toward public servant* to pay a fine or to imprisonment for at most six months.

If the crime is grave, imprisonment for at most four years shall be imposed.

Sec. 3. The provisions of Sections 1 and 2 shall also apply, if a person, in a manner mentioned in said paragraphs, attacks one who is or has been called to assist an official there mentioned in a function.

Sec. 4. Even though no case previously referred to in this Chapter is involved, a person, who makes resistance or otherwise seeks to prevent the exercise of a function referred to in Section 1, shall be sentenced for *violent resistance* to pay a fine or to imprisonment for at most six months.

Sec. 5. If some one insults a person, who enjoys protection in accord with Section 1, during or because of such person's function, he shall be sentenced for *insulting a public servant* to pay a fine or to imprisonment for at most six months.

Sec. 6. If a person spreads among people a false rumor or other untrue assertion likely to undermine respect for an authority or other organ entitled to make decisions in public matters, he shall be sentenced for *calumniating authority* to pay a fine or to imprisonment for at most two years.

Sec. 7. A person, who gives, promises or offers a bribe or other illicit reward for the exercise of a function carrying official responsibility, shall be sentenced for *bribery* to pay a fine or to imprisonment for at most two years.

Sec. 8. A person, who, at an election to public office or in connection with some other exercise of suffrage in public matters, attempts to prevent voting or to tamper with its outcome or otherwise improperly to influence the vote, shall be sentenced for *improper activity at election* to pay a fine or to imprisonment for at most six months.

If the crime is grave, imprisonment for at most four years shall be imposed. In judging the gravity of the crime, special attention shall be paid to whether it had been committed by use of violence or threat of violence or had involved misuse of an official position.

A person, who receives, accepts a promise of, or demands an illicit favor for voting in a certain manner or for abstaining from voting on a public matter, shall be sentenced, unless it is a crime in office, for *accepting an illicit reward for voting* to pay a fine or to imprisonment for at most six months.

Sec. 9. If a person without authorization seeks to secure information about matters which, with respect to the exercise of suffrage on public questions shall be kept secret, he shall be sentenced for *violating the privacy of suffrage* to pay a fine or to imprisonment for at most six months.

Sec. 10. A person, who, by violence or threat of violence, attacks some one because he has, in court or before another authority, filed a complaint, brought suit, testified, or else made a statement at a hearing, or to prevent him from so doing, shall be sentenced for *interference in a judicial matter* to pay a fine or to imprisonment for at most two years. The same shall apply, if a person by some other act which causes suffering, injury or inconvenience, or by threat of such act, attacks some one because he had testified or made other statement at an official hearing, or does so to prevent him from making such statement.

Sec. 11. If a person hides some one who has committed a crime, helps him to escape, destroys evidence of the crime, or in other like ways thwarts its discovery or prosecution, he shall be sentenced for *protecting a criminal* to pay a fine or to imprisonment for at most two years.

A person, who did not realize but had reasonable grounds to assume that the other was a criminal, shall be sentenced to pay a fine.

Punishment shall not be imposed, in accord with this Section, on a spouse, betrothed, sibling, relative in ascending or descending line, one by marriage equally closely related to the criminal, foster parents or foster children. As amended, SFS 1971:874, eff. January 1, 1972.

Sec. 12. If a person assists some one, who is a convicted prisoner, or committed to jail, or arrested or otherwise deprived of his liberty for reason other than medical care or care in accord with the Child Welfare Act or the Temperance Act, to gain his freedom, or after such escape aids him by hiding him or by other like action, he shall be sentenced for *aiding escape* to pay a fine or to imprisonment for at most two years.

Sec. 13. A person, who violates an order prohibiting the sale or dispersion of goods or the dispensing of another's goods, moves property that has been sequestrated, distrained or confiscated; injures or removes an official notice or seal or otherwise unlawfully opens something officially closed, or breaks some other similar officially proclaimed order, shall be sentenced for *violation of official order* to pay a fine or to imprisonment for at most one year.

If a person refuses admission which an official functionary may demand, he shall be sentenced for *obstructing official function* to pay a fine.

Sec. 14. If a person, without authorization, performs what pertains to an office carrying official responsibility, he shall be sentenced for *unauthorized performance of official duty* to pay a fine or to imprisonment for at most six months.

If the crime is regarded as grave because the offender wanted to obtain unauthorized gains or for other reason, imprisonment for at most four years shall be imposed.

Sec. 15. Even though no case mentioned in Section 14 is involved, a person, who, without authorization, claims to be holding the office there mentioned, shall be sentenced for *alleging a public office* to pay a fine or to imprisonment for at most six months. The same shall apply, if a person without authorization wears a uniform, symbol or other service token which makes him appear to belong to the armed services or some other branch of public service or to a service dealing with public communications or the supply of water, light, heat or power to the public.

If a person without authorization claims to be an attorney, he shall be sentenced for *pretending to be an attorney* to pay a fine.

Sec. 16. Attempt or preparation to commit violence or threat to a public servant shall be punished as stated in Chapter 23, unless the crime would have been considered petty, had it been completed. Attempt to aid escape shall also be punished as stated in Chapter 23.

CHAPTER 18

Of Crimes of Lese-Majesty

Sec. 1. A person, who, with intent that the form of government be overthrown by force of arms or other violent means or that a measure or decision of the King, the Parliament or the Supreme Court be thus extorted or prevented, takes action which dangerously favors the realization of such intent, shall, if it is not high treason, be sentenced for *sedition* to imprisonment for ten years, or for life or, if the danger is minor, for at least four and at most ten years.

Sec. 2. If the act referred to in Chapters 3–5 involves an offense against the King or other member of the Royal family or against a Regent serving in place of the King, imprisonment for at most four years shall be imposed if otherwise at most six months' imprisonment can be imposed for the crime, and for at most six years, if the crime otherwise would be punishable by imprisonment for more than six months but at most four years.

Sec. 3. A person who, with the intent that the crime be committed against public security or the liberty of citizens, gathers or leads an armed force or keeps it assembled or furnishes a force with arms, ammunition or other like equipment or trains it in the use of arms, shall be sentenced for *armed threat against the legal order* to imprisonment for at least six and at most ten years.

Sec. 4. If a person organizes or participates in an association, which must be considered to constitute or, in view of its character and the purpose for which it has been organized, is easily capable of developing into an instrument of force, such as a military troop or a police force, and which does not with due permission strengthen the defense establishment or the police, or who on behalf of such association is concerned with arms, ammunition or other like equipment makes available a building or land for its activity or supports it with money or in other ways, shall be sentenced for *unlawful military activity* to pay a fine or to imprisonment for at most two years.

Sec. 5. A person, who exerts illegal coercion or illegal threat with the intent of influencing the shaping of public opinion or of encroaching on the freedom of action within a political organization or a trade or industrial association and thereby endangers freedom of speech, assembly or association, shall be sentenced for *crime against civil liberty* to imprisonment for at most six years.

Sec. 6. If a person, by mutilation or otherwise, for a short or long period incapacitates himself for military service which it was his duty to discharge in the armed forces or otherwise for the defense of the Realm, or by feigning illness or by means of other deception shirks such service, he shall be sentenced for *evading defense duty* to pay a fine or to imprisonment for at most two years or, if the country was at war, to pay a fine or to imprisonment for at most four years.

Sec. 7. Attempt, preparation or conspiracy to commit sedition or armed threat against the legal order, failure to reveal such crime, as well as attempt to commit crime against civil liberty, or evading defense duty shall be punished as stated in Chapter 23.

Sec. 8. An act referred to in Chapters 3–5 which involves an offense against the King or some one else mentioned in Section 2 may not be prosecuted by the public prosecutor without an order from the King, unless some one died as a result of the act. The same shall apply with respect to attempt, preparation or conspiracy to commit an act just mentioned or failure to reveal such act.

CHAPTER 19

Of Crimes Against the Security of the Realm

Sec. 1. A person, who with the intent that the Realm or a part thereof, by violent or otherwise illegal means or with foreign aid, be placed under foreign domination or made dependent on a foreign power, or that a part of the Realm be thus torn loose, takes action which dangerously favors the realization of such intent shall be sentenced for *high treason* to imprisonment for ten years or for life or, if the danger was minor, for at least four and at most ten years.

If a person, with the intent that a measure or decision of the King, Parliament or the Supreme Court be extorted or prevented with foreign assistance, engages in an act that involves a danger of this occurring, he shall also be sentenced for high treason.

Sec. 2. A person, who by violent means or foreign aid produces a danger of the Realm's being involved in war or other hostilities, shall, unless it is high treason, be sentenced for *instigating war* to imprisonment for at least two and at most eight years.

Sec. 3. If a person, who has received a commission to negotiate with a foreign power or otherwise to protect the concerns of the Realm, in being with some one who represents the interests of a foreign power misuses his authority to represent the Realm or otherwise his position of trust and thereby causes the Realm considerable harm, he shall be sentenced for *disloyalty in negotiation with a foreign power* to imprisonment for a fixed term of at least two and at most ten years, or for life.

Sec. 4. A Swedish citizen, who, lacking permission from the King or his deputy, lets himself be used as an agent of a foreign power in a diplomatic matter which concerns the Realm, as well as any one, who in the alleged capacity of an authorized agent enters into negotiation about such a matter with some one who represents the interests of a foreign power, shall be sentenced for *arbitrary conduct in negotiation with a foreign power* to imprisonment for at most two years or, if the country was at war, for at most four years.

If the crime contained a danger for the country's right of selfdetermination or its peaceful relations with a foreign power, imprisonment for at least one and at most six years shall be imposed or, if the country was at war, for a fixed term of at least four and at most ten years, or for life.

Sec. 5. A person, who, with the intent of aiding a foreign power, without authorization obtains, transmits, gives or otherwise reveals information concerning a defense facility, arms, supplies, imports, exports or other conditions, the disclosure of which to a foreign power can bring harm to the defense of the Realm, to the provisioning of the people during war or during extraordinary conditions caused by war, or otherwise to the security of the Realm, shall be sentenced, whether the information is correct or not, for *espionage* to imprisonment for at most six years. The same shall apply, if a person, with the intent just mentioned, without authorization produces or is concerned with a writing, drawing or other object containing such information.

Sec. 6. If a crime referred to in Section 5 is regarded as grave, imprisonment for a fixed term of at least four and at most ten years, or for life, shall be imposed for *grave espionage.*

In judging the gravity of the crime, special attention shall be paid to whether the act was of a significantly dangerous nature in view of ongoing war or concerned matters of great importance or whether the criminal revealed something entrusted to him because of his position in public or private service.

Sec. 7. If with respect to information concerning matters of a secret nature, the act referred to in Section 5 is committed without intent to aid a foreign power, a sentence to pay a fine or to imprisonment for at most two years or, if the country was at war, to pay a fine or to imprisonment for at most four years shall be imposed for *unauthorized dealing with secret information.*

A person, who, due to gross carelessness, transmits, gives or otherwise reveals information referred to in Section 5 and concerning matters of a secret nature, shall be sentenced for *carelessness with secret information* to pay a fine or to imprisonment for at most six months or, if the country was at war, to pay a fine or to imprisonment for at most two years.

Sec. 8. If a person spreads among people or communicates to or allows a false rumor or other untrue assertion, apt to produce a danger for the security of the Realm, to reach a foreign power, he shall be sentenced for *trafficking in rumor endangering the security of the Realm* to pay a fine or to imprisonment for at most two years.

A person, who, with the intent of aiding a foreign power, carries on an activity in this Realm for obtaining information about military or other matters, the revealing of which to the foreign power can produce harm to the security of another foreign power, or who lends to such activity within the Realm a cooperation which is not merely incidental, shall be sentenced for *unlawful informational activity* to pay a fine or to imprisonment for at most two years.

A sentence for unlawful informational activity shall also be imposed if a person, with the intent of aiding a foreign power, secretly or by the use of fraudulent means, within this Realm either carries on activity for obtaining information about another's personal affairs or lends to such activity a cooperation which is not merely incidental.

Sec. 10. Repealed, SFS 1970:225, eff. February 17, 1971 (SFS 1971:29).

Sec. 11. If an act referred to in Chapter 3 or 4 implies that a person, by an offense against a foreign power's chief of state or its representative in this Realm, affronts the foreign power, imprisonment for at most two years shall be imposed, if the crime otherwise can be punished by imprisonment for at most six months, and for at most four years, if otherwise the crime is punishable by imprisonment for more than six months and at most two years. What has just been stated shall have corresponding application, if a foreign power is affronted because someone intrudes in premises occupied by its representatives or causes damage to such premises or to property therein contained. As amended, SFS 1970:225, eff. July 1, 1970.

Sec. 12. If a person within this Realm and without the permission of the King recruits people for foreign military service or service comparable to it or induces people to leave the country unlawfully in order to enter such service, he shall be sentenced for *unlawful recruiting* to pay a fine or to imprisonment for at most six months or, if the country was at war, to imprisonment for at most two years.

Sec. 13. A person, who accepts money or other property from a foreign power or from some one acting in its interest, for the purpose of influencing public opinion concerning the form of government or governmental measures in domestic or foreign affairs by issuing or distributing writings or by other means, shall be sentenced for *accepting foreign aid* to imprisonment for at most two years.

Sec. 14. Attempt, preparation or conspiracy to commit high treason, disloyalty in negotiation with foreign power, espionage, grave espionage, or unlawful informational activity, as well as attempt or preparation to engage in unauthorized dealing with secret information, shall be punished as stated in Chapter 23. Making contact with a foreign power for the purpose of preparing, making possible or facilitating high treason shall also be regarded as conspiracy to commit such crime.

A person who fails to reveal high treason, disloyalty in negotiation with a foreign power, espionage or grave espionage, shall also be punished as stated in Chapter 23; he shall be so punished even though he did not realize but should have realized that a crime was being committed.

Sec. 15. If a person, who, in view of what is known to him, on the basis of warnings given or otherwise should have realized that high treason, disloyalty in negotiation with a foreign power, espionage or grave espionage is going on, contributes to the act, he shall be punished as though he were an accessory; however, no more severe punishment than imprisonment for two years may be imposed.

Sec. 16. Unlawful informational activity or unlawful recruiting, or attempt, preparation or conspiracy to undertake unlawful informational activity may not be prosecuted by the public prosecutor without an order from the King. As amended, SFS 1970:225, eff. February 17, 1971 (SFS 1971:29).

An act referred to in Chapters 3 or 4 and involving such affront to a foreign power as is mentioned in Section 11; as well as attempt, preparation or conspiracy to commit such act or failure to reveal such act, are not subject to public prosecution without an order from the King or from one authorized by the King. As amended, SFS 1970:225, eff. July 1, 1970.

CHAPTER 20

Of Crimes in Office

Sec. 1. If a civil servant, by act of commission or omission, misuses his position to the detriment of the public or of some individual, he shall, if the act does not constitute embezzlement or other breach of trust or else is separately made subject to punishment, be sentenced for *misuse of office* to suspension or dismissal; if appropriate reasons exist, he shall also be sentenced to imprisonment for at most two years. In petty cases only a fine shall be imposed.

If the crime is grave, dismissal and imprisonment for at most six years shall be imposed.

Sec. 2. A civil servant, who accepts, takes a promise of, or demands a bribe or other illicit reward for his official service, shall, if the act is not otherwise separately made subject to punishment, be sentenced as provided in Section 1 for *taking a bribe or other illicit reward.* The same shall apply, if he committed such offense before he received his post.

If a person who has been a civil servant commits an act described in the first paragraph, he shall be sentenced to pay a fine or to imprisonment as provided in Section 1.

Sec. 3. If a civil servant discloses what he is in duty bound to keep secret or if he unlawfully makes use of such secret, he shall, if the act is not otherwise separately made subject to punishment, be sentenced to suspension or dismissal for *violation of duty to maintain silence;* if appropriate reasons exist, he shall also be sentenced to imprisonment for at most one year. In petty cases only a fine shall be imposed.

If a person who has been a civil servant commits such act, he shall be sentenced to pay a fine or to imprisonment as provided in the first paragraph.

Sec. 4. If a civil servant, out of neglect, ignorance or incompetence disregards what is incumbent upon him in conformity with law, instructions or other ordinance, special directive, or the nature of his office, he shall, if the act does not constitute misuse of office or is otherwise separately made subject to punishment, be sentenced for *breach of official duty* to pay a fine or to suspension.

If the breach is grave, he shall be sentenced to suspension or dismissal; if appropriate reasons exist, he shall also be sentenced to imprisonment for at most one year.

Participation in a strike or similar concerted activity pursuant to a decision of a union which organized the activity shall not under any circumstances be construed as breach of official duty. As amended, SFS 1965:280, eff. January 1, 1966.

Sec. 5. If a civil servant is found to have disregarded his official duty by an act made punishable elsewhere than in Sections 1–4, imprisonment for at most two years may be imposed even though such a severe punishment otherwise could not have followed.

Sec. 6. If a person, who according to the provisions of Sections 1–4 has incurred liability to suspension or dismissal from a given office, no longer holds the same office but has instead received another post with similar duties, he shall be sentenced to suspension or dismissal from that post.

If he has not, in lieu of his office, received another post as stated in the first paragraph, he shall be sentenced to pay a fine or to imprisonment in accord with provisions in Sections 1–4. If otherwise he should have been sentenced to suspension or dismissal together with fine or imprisonment, the fixing of the punishment may be made with due consideration of the fact that suspension or dismissal is not being imposed. If he should not have been sentenced to any sanction other than suspension or dismissal, he may be absolved of all sanction.

Sec. 7. When a person, who, in accord with provisions in Sections 1–4 is sentenced to or has incurred liability to suspension or dismissal from office, occupies another office carrying official responsibility that one referred to in the first paragraph of Section 6, he shall be dismissed from that office, if the crime has shown him to be obviously unfit to retain it. If he has otherwise in a noteworthy degree damaged the reputation which the holder of the office should possess, he shall be sentenced to suspension from that office.

If a person who is punished in accord with Section 2, second paragraph, or Section 3, second paragraph, occupies a post carrying official responsibility, the provisions of the first paragraph above shall apply correspondingly.

Sec. 8. If a civil servant has, by a crime other than one referred to in Sections 1–4, shown himself to be obviously unfit to occupy his posts, he shall, in addition to any other sanction that should be imposed, be sentenced to dismissal. However, if the crime is not punishable by imprisonment for two years or longer, dismissal may be imposed only if the special character of the office requires it.

If a civil servant is not sentenced to dismissal in conformity with the first paragraph, he shall be sentenced to suspension from his post, if by his crime he has in a noteworthy degree damaged the reputation which the occupant of the post should possess.

When suspension or dismissal is imposed in conformity with this Section, the loss which the civil servant suffers thereby shall be taken into consideration in fixing other sanction for the crime; thus a fine or disciplinary punishment which otherwise should have been imposed may be completely remitted.

Sec. 9. If an administrative agency has imposed a disciplinary punishment on a civil servant for a given crime, a court must take this into consideration when fixing a sanction for the same crime and may completely remit fine, disciplinary punishment or suspension which otherwise should have been imposed. The decision of the administrative agency shall be vacated, if it has not been fully or partially executed when prosecution for the crime is instituted.

Sec. 10. If a civil servant has stayed away from his post without permission or previously announced excuse and it has been impossible to locate him in order to serve a summons or bring him to court, he shall, unless he appears before the expiration of three months from the date the summons issued to him by the court was inserted in the public newspapers, be sentenced to dismissal from his post.

Sec. 11. If a person has been accessory to misuse of office, the taking of a bribe or illicit reward, or a breach of duty to maintain silence, without in so doing neglecting his official duties, he shall, in conformity with the provisions in Chapter 23, be sentenced to pay a fine or to imprisonment in accord with the provisions in Section 1, 2, or 3 above. If he himself is a civil servant, the provisions of Section 8 shall be applied also.

A sentence for accessory to breach of official duty may be imposed only upon a person who, in so doing, neglected an official duty.

Sec. 12. As used in this Code, the term civil servant means a judge, other state official who can be dismissed from office only by the sentence of a court, as well as a person who holds a position of trust from which the King may remove him. What is said of civil servants shall also apply to persons charged with the administration of the affairs of city, community or public funds, departments or other institutions or foundations approved by the King, to employees of civil service or administrative authorities, and to others who have been commissioned to serve in an official capacity or to perform an official duty.

A person who is appointed or elected a member of a decision-making state or communal assembly or who sits on a jury or a board of taxation shall also be subject to official responsibility in terms of Sections 2, 3, and 5–8, but suspension may not be imposed, nor may a person, who is an elected member of a decision-making state or communal assembly, be sentenced to dismissal in accord with Section 8 except when he has committed a crime punishable by imprisonment for two years or longer. The provisions of Section 3 shall also apply to a person who is employed in public service or in performing a legally defined official duty but who is not subject to official responsibility.

The provisions of Sections 2 and 3 concerning a person who has been a civil servant shall apply correspondingly to a person who has been subject to responsibility as stated in the second paragraph.

Sec. 13. If a person holding an office in an enterprise of public communication, which according to the King's decree shall enjoy the protection mentioned in Chapter 17, Section 1, neglects to do what is incumbent upon him for the prevention of an accident, the provisions of Sections 5 and 8 shall apply.

Sec. 14. Regardless of what the law may otherwise provide, the public prosecutor may prosecute a crime by which a civil servant has neglected his official duty; however, the provisions of this Code shall apply, namely that prosecution may not be instituted without an order from the King or from one authorized by the King, and the provisions of other laws or statutes shall apply concerning the prosecution of an act referred to in Section 3 and separately made subject to punishment, or an act made punishable only when committed by a civil servant.

Sec. 15. If, before the imposition of sentence or later but before the sentence became definitive, a person convicted of crime has been appointed, or, subsequent to an election within the period stated, chosen for an office, and if the court has not considered the matter of his suspension or dismissal from said office in accord with Sections 6, 7, or 8, a separate action for suspension or dismissal may be brought. However, such action shall be brought within two years from the time the sentence became definitive or the votes were counted, if the counting after election occurred after the sentence had become definitive.

CHAPTER 21

Of Crimes by Members of the Armed Services

Sec. 1. If a serviceman refuses or fails to obey the order of a superior or unduly delays the fulfillment of the order and if it is not obvious that the order is not related to the service, he shall be sentenced for *disobedience* to a disciplinary punishment or to imprisonment for at most one year.

Sec. 2. If the crime referred to in Section 1 is regarded as grave, imprisonment for at most four years shall be imposed for *grave disobedience.* In judging the gravity of the crime, special attention shall be paid to whether the order concerned a service measure of considerable importance or the crime had occurred in the presence of an assembled troop or had been committed by several in concert.

If the country was at war or if the crime was committed during combat or else on an occasion when a crime against military discipline incurs a special danger, imprisonment for at most ten years, or for life, shall be imposed.

Sec. 3. If a gathering of servicemen displays an intention to rise against a superior by joint force, sentences shall be imposed for *mutiny;* on instigator and leader, to imprisonment for at most six years and on other participant to disciplinary punishment or to imprisonment for at most four years.

If participants in a mutiny have together inflicted violence on person or property, instigator and leader shall be sentenced to imprisonment for at most ten years, or for life, and other participant to imprisonment for at most six years.

If mutiny occurs when the country is at war or if it happens during combat or else on an occasion when a crime against military discipline incurs a special danger, imprisonment for at most ten years, or for life, shall be imposed.

Sec. 4. If a serviceman does not comply with an order given by a sentry or other serviceman assigned to guard duty or the maintenance of order, in connection with such duty, he shall be sentenced for *disobeying a guard* to disciplinary punishment or to imprisonment for at most one year.

If the crime is grave, imprisonment for at most four years shall be imposed.

Sec. 5. If a superior abuses his authority by seeking to persuade a subordinate to do something which it is not the latter's duty to do, suffer, or omit to do, he shall be sentenced for *abuse of authority* to disciplinary punishment or to imprisonment for at most one year.

The same shall apply, if a superior improperly, because of

the subordinate's condition in or outside the service, makes him perform special tasks or refuses him a benefit and also if a superior for no reason exposes a subordinate to a danger to his life or health.

If the crime is grave, imprisonment for at most four years shall be imposed.

Sec. 6. A serviceman, who, without authority to do so, gives orders to another serviceman, shall be sentenced for ***unauthorized exercise of command*** to disciplinary punishment or to imprisonment for at most one year.

If the crime is grave, imprisonment for at most four years shall be imposed.

Sec. 7. If a serviceman, by violence or threat of violence, attacks a serviceman who is on duty, or does so in order to compel him to perform or prevent him from performing a service task, or otherwise on account of his service, he shall be sentenced for ***violence or threat against a serviceman*** to disciplinary punishment or to imprisonment for at most two years or, if the crime is petty, to disciplinary punishment or to imprisonment for at most six months. If the crime is regarded as grave, in that it involved threat to military discipline or otherwise, imprisonment for at most four years shall be imposed.

If, while the country is at war, a serviceman commits a crime just mentioned against a superior or against a sentry or other serviceman assigned to guard duty or the maintenance of order, he shall be sentenced to imprisonment for at most ten years or, if the crime is petty, to disciplinary punishment or to imprisonment for at most six months. If it occurs during combat or else on an occasion when a crime against military discipline incurs a special danger, imprisonment for life may be imposed.

Sec. 8. A serviceman who insults another serviceman, during or because of the latter's service, shall be sentenced for ***insulting a serviceman*** to disciplinary punishment or to imprisonment for at most six months.

Sec. 9. If a serviceman, in a case other than one previously mentioned, shows disrespect for a superior or disdain for a subordinate or in other ways lacks in proper conduct toward a serviceman, and it happens during or because of the latter's service, he shall be sentenced for *improper conduct* to disciplinary punishment.

Sec. 10. A serviceman who orally before a gathering of servicemen incites or otherwise seeks to provoke a crime of disobedience or other act, by which a serviceman overlooks his service duty, shall be sentenced for *inciting servicemen to rebellion* to disciplinary punishment or to imprisonment for at most one year.

If the crime is regarded as grave because the offender had tried to provoke a serious crime or otherwise, imprisonment for at most four years shall be imposed.

Sec. 11. If a serviceman unlawfully absconds or stays away from a detachment of the military forces in which he is to serve or stay or, if he is to serve elsewhere than in a detachment of the military forces, from the place of such service, he shall be sentenced for *absence without leave* to disciplinary punishment or to imprisonment for at most six months.

Absence without leave during a period of emergency or while the country is at war shall be punished by disciplinary punishment or imprisonment for at most two years.

Sec. 12. If, with regard to the period during which the offender stayed away or intended to absent himself, or the nature of his service duties, his absence without leave has caused or could have caused a substantial interruption of his training or other considerable harm to the service, he shall be sentenced for *desertion* to disciplinary punishment or to imprisonment for at most two years.

Desertion during a period of emergency shall be punished by imprisonment for at most two years. If the country was at war, imprisonment for at most ten years shall be imposed.

Sec. 13. If a serviceman, who serves as chief of a detachment of the military forces or performs guard duty or similar task, leaves his post without permission or if through the consumption of alcoholic beverages or otherwise he is found to have rendered himself incapable of discharging his duties, he shall be sentenced for *abandoning post* to disciplinary punishment or to imprisonment for at most two years.

Abandoning a post while the country is at war shall be punished by disciplinary punishment or imprisonment for at most four years; if the crime was committed during combat or else on an occasion when a crime against military discipline incurs a special danger, imprisonment for at most ten years, or for life, shall be imposed.

Sec. 14. If, while performing his duties, a serviceman is so under the influence of alcoholic beverages or other intoxicant that his ability to perform his duty must be assumed to be diminished, he shall be sentenced for *intoxication while performing a duty* to disciplinary punishment or to imprisonment for at most one year.

Sec. 15. A serviceman, who, within an area or space used by the military forces, appears intoxicated by alcoholic beverages, as evidenced by his gestures or speech, shall be sentenced for *drunkenness* to disciplinary punishment.

Disciplinary punishment shall also be imposed, if the intoxication was caused by something other than alcoholic beverages.

Sec. 16. A serviceman who, within an area or space used by the military forces, is boisterous or otherwise behaves in a manner apt to arouse general indignation, shall be sentenced for *disorderly conduct* to disciplinary punishment.

Sec. 17. If a serviceman, who is not subject to official responsibility, by act or failure to act misuses his position to the detriment of the military forces or else of the community or of an individual, he shall, if the act is not separately made subject to punishment, be sentenced for *misuse of office* to imprisonment for at most two years or, if the crime is petty, to disciplinary punishment.

Sec. 18. If a serviceman, who is not subject to official responsibility, by neglect, lack of understanding or skill disregards what is incumbent on him according to regulations, instructions or other general prescriptions, special directives or the nature of his service, he shall, if the act does not constitute misuse of office or else is separately made subject to punishment, be sentenced for *breach of official duty* to disciplinary punishment. The provisions of Chapter 20, Section 4, paragraph 3 shall have corresponding application with respect to professional servicemen.

If the breach is grave, imprisonment for at most one year shall be imposed. As amended, SFS 1965:280, eff. January 1, 1966.

Sec. 19. Preparation, conspiracy or failure to reveal mutiny, and also attempt, preparation or conspiracy or failure to reveal desertion during a period of emergency or war shall be punished as stated in Chapter 23. The same shall apply to attempt at, preparation or conspiracy to commit violence or threat against a serviceman, unless the crime, had it been completed, would have been regarded as petty.

As accessory to breach of official duties, only that person shall be punished who thereby has set aside an official duty.

Sec. 20. According to this Code, servicemen are those who as officers, warrant officers, noncommissioned officers or privates are employed in the military forces and draftees who have not received permission for weapon-free service and members or recruits of the homeguard, all together during the period they are bound to serve in such capacity. To the extent that the King so directs, in view of the need of officers and other service conditions, those who are otherwise employed in the military forces or have committed themselves to enter the military service as volunteers are also servicemen during the period they are subject to military duty in such capacity. If someone is on leave not limited to less than two months, he is not regarded as being on military duty. More specific provisions as to what is meant by the military forces are issued by the King.

Those referred to in the first paragraph shall, besides the period when they are subject to military duty, be regarded as servicemen when in connection with such period they are under care in a military hospital, when they are inmates of a military jail and when they within an area or space used by the military forces or otherwise publicly appear in a service uniform, as well as with reference to the performance of their duty to report or some other particular service duty.

A serviceman, who has the right of command over another serviceman, is the latter's superior. A serviceman, over whom another serviceman has the right of command, is subordinate to the latter. As amended, SFS 1966:415, eff. Oct. 1, 1966.

Sec. 21. Of the personnel mentioned in Section 20, first paragraph, officers, warrant officers and other officers of no lower rank than a sergeant and those who hold a corresponding service position shall be subject to official responsibility, whether they are in active service or not.

Sec. 22. Provisions of Chapter 20, Section 14, shall have corresponding application with respect to crime by which a serviceman has set aside his official duty.

CHAPTER 22

Articles of War

Sec. 1. A person, who, when the country is at war,

1. obstructs, misleads or betrays servicemen or others active in the defense of the Realm or seduces them to mutiny, or to be disloyal or spiritless;

2. betrays, destroys or damages fortification, war supplies, factory, depot, power installation, traffic artery, vessel or other things of importance for the defense or for public subsistence;

3. by untrue representation spreads distrust among the public,

4. procures for the enemy military manpower, equipment, provisions or support; or

5. commits any other similar treasonable act,

shall, if the act is likely to result in considerable harm to the military forces of the Realm or otherwise to the defense of the Realm or to the provisioning of the public or involves considerable aid to the enemy, be sentenced for *treason* to imprisonment for a fixed term of at least four and at most ten years, or for life.

If the act referred to in the first paragraph is only to a lesser degree likely to result in harm to the defense of the Realm or to the provisioning of the public or involves a lesser aid to the enemy, than there stated, imprisonment for at most six years shall be imposed for *treachery.* If the act consisted of furnishing of equipment or provisions or of some other service to the enemy within an area occupied by him and if, considering the needs of the population, the offender's livelihood or other special circumstances, the act could not be regarded as inappropriate, no punishment shall be imposed.

Sec. 2. If a person due to carelessness commits an act referred to in Section 1, he shall be sentenced for *carelessness harmful to the country* to imprisonment for at most four years.

Sec. 3. A serviceman, who, when the country is at war, deserts to the enemy or otherwise voluntarily surrenders to him, shall be sentenced for *desertion to the enemy* to imprisonment for a fixed term of at least four and at most ten years, or for life.

The same shall apply if, when the country is at war, a Swedish citizen bears arms against the Realm and such act is not considered to be treason.

Sec. 4. A serviceman, who, when the country is at war, without authorization sends a message to or otherwise enters into contact with some one belonging to the enemy's military forces or stays within the enemy area, shall be sentenced for *consorting with the enemy* to disciplinary punishment or to imprisonment for at most two years.

Sec. 5. If, when the country is at war, a serviceman, during combat or else on an occasion when a crime against military discipline produces a special danger, advises servicemen to surrender to the enemy, or otherwise in the presence of servicemen without authorization does something likely to provoke disloyalty or lack of spirit, he shall be sentenced for *undermining the will to fight* to imprisonment for a fixed term of at least four and at most ten years, or for life. If the danger was slight, imprisonment for at most six years shall be imposed.

Sec. 6. A serviceman, who, when the country is at war, spreads among servicemen a false rumor or other untrue assertion likely to promote disloyalty or lack of spirit, shall be sentenced for *spreading rumor harmful to defense* to disciplinary punishment or to imprisonment for at most two years.

Sec. 7. If, during a state of emergency or when the country is at war, servicemen unauthorizedly hold a meeting on a topic the discussion of which can easily lead to disobedience or desertion or to the spreading of fear or distrust among the servicemen, the participant shall be sentenced for *unlawful assembly* to disciplinary punishment or to imprisonment for at most two years. A person, who participated at the instigation of or by permission of a superior shall be free of punishment.

Sec. 8. If, during a state of emergency or when the country is at war, a serviceman intentionally or through carelessness neglects what pertains to him to do to make a defense installation ready for combat, bring a detachment to combat readiness, procure provisions or otherwise prepare a war enterprise, he shall be sentenced for *neglect of war preparation* to imprisonment for at most six years.

If an intentionally committed crime just mentioned is regarded as grave, considering that the success of a war enterprise was endangered thereby or for other reasons, imprisonment for a fixed term of at least four and at most ten years, or for life, shall be imposed.

Sec. 9. If, when the country is at war, a serviceman who serves as head of a detachment of the armed forces, without exploiting available ways and means of defense, taking prescribed demolition measures or carrying out specially ordered resistance, surrenders to the enemy a combat position, war material or other things having considerable value for warfare, or surrenders himself or his detachment to the enemy, shall be sentenced for *capitulation* to imprisonment for a fixed term of at least six and at most ten years, or for life.

Sec. 10. If, when the country is at war, a serviceman intentionally or from carelessness, during or in connection with combat, fails to perform to the utmost his duty to further the conduct of the war, he shall be sentenced for *combat neglect* to imprisonment for at most six years.

If an intentionally committed crime just mentioned is regarded as grave, considering that the success of a war enterprise was endangered thereby, the offender occupied a responsible post, or for other reasons, imprisonment for a fixed term of at least four and at most ten years, or for life, shall be imposed.

Sec. 11. A person, who in the conduct of war, by using means of warfare likely to cause unnecessary suffering or by misusing the Red Cross sign, or otherwise, acts in a manner contrary to existing treaties with foreign powers or to generally recognized principles of international law, shall be sentenced for *crime against international law* to imprisonment for at most four years; if the crime is petty, a fine shall be imposed or, if he is a serviceman, disciplinary punishment. A person shall also be sentenced for crime against international law if in a case other than in warfare he ignores what according to such treaties or principles must be observed with reference to protection of the wounded, ill or shipwrecked of the combat forces in the field or at sea, prisoners of war or civilian population during wartime, or otherwise pertaining to occupation, and thereby causes injury to person, bodily or mental suffering or else other harm or inconvenience which is not slight.

If the crime is grave, imprisonment for a fixed term of at least two and at most ten years, or for life, shall be imposed. In judging the gravity of the crime special attention shall be paid to whether it had been committed through a large number of diverse acts or else many persons had been killed or injured thereby or extensive loss of property had ensued.

Sec. 12. Attempt, preparation or conspiracy to commit treason, treachery or desertion to the enemy shall be punished as provided in Chapter 23. Consorting with the enemy in order to prepare, make possible or facilitate the commission of a crime just mentioned shall also be regarded as conspiracy. Punishment for preparation or conspiracy during a time when the country is threatened by war, occupation or other hostilities shall be imposed even though hostilities have not opened.

A person who fails to reveal treason, treachery or desertion to the enemy, shall also be punished as stated in Chapter 23; and such punishment shall be imposed even if he had not understood but should have understood that the crime was occurring.

Sec. 13. If during warfare a crime has been committed by someone who in so doing had not lacked reason to suppose that the act was permissible in accord with customs of warfare, a lesser punishment may be imposed than that provided for the act. If the circumstances are greatly extenuating, no punishment shall be imposed.

Sec. 14. During a state of emergency and when the country is at war, in addition to a person who on account of Chapter 21, Section 20 or of prescriptions based thereon is a serviceman, everybody who is obligated to serve in the armed forces shall also be regarded as a serviceman, to the extent that the King does not decree otherwise. That which has been said about a serviceman shall, when the country is at war, have corresponding application to a policeman, who although not being obligated to serve in the military forces is duty bound to participate in the defense of the Realm, to a person who has to perform police work necessary for the protection of certain property and thereby belongs to the armed forces in accord with Royal decree; as well as to a person who belongs to a branch of civil defense, the personnel of which is obligated, in accord with Royal decree, to perform work which rests on the military forces.

A person who otherwise, during a state of emergency or when the country is at war, is staying with a detachment of the military forces which is in the field of combat or serves under similar conditions, shall also be regarded as a serviceman.

The provisions governing servicemen shall in applicable parts apply to a prisoner of war, a war participant who has been interned during a war in which the Realm is neutral, and a foreigner who is staying with prisoners of war or interned war participants for the purpose of rendering medical or spiritual care.

Sec. 15. If, when the country is at war, an act referred to in Chapter 21 or in this Chapter is committed against a State allied with the Realm, against the military forces of such State or against some one belonging to them, the provisions of law governing the same acts against the Realm, its military forces or a serviceman shall have corresponding application.

Sec. 16. To the extent that it is found necessary, in view of danger of war in which the Realm finds itself or other extraordinary conditions due to war, the King may decree that the provisions of Chapters 19 and 21 and of this Chapter in case the country is at war shall in applicable parts also govern with respect to crime committed at another time.

If the country should happen to be wholly or partly occupied by a foreign power without the occurrence of military resistance, the applicable parts of the provisions of said chapters relevant in case the country is at war shall likewise apply to crime committed during such period. In that connection that which is stated about the defense of the Realm shall be applicable to the resistance activity and what is stated about the enemy shall be applicable to the occupying power.

Sec. 17. In this Chapter a foreign power with which the country is not at war is equated with an enemy if there is danger that war with that power may break out.

Sec. 18. Concerning the beginning and the cessation of a state of emergency, special provisions are made.

Sec. 19. When the country is at war, death penalty may be applied in certain cases. This is dealt with in a special statute.

CHAPTER 23

Of Attempt, Preparation, Conspiracy and Complicity

Sec. 1. If some one has begun to commit a given crime without its arriving at completion, he shall, in cases where specific provisions have been made governing this, be sentenced for attempt to commit the crime, if there had been a danger that the act would lead to the completion of the crime or such danger had been precluded only because of accidental circumstances.

Punishment for attempt shall be fixed at most at what applies to a completed crime and not at less than imprisonment, if the lowest punishment for the completed crime is imprisonment for two years or more.

Sec. 2. A person who, with the intention of committing or promoting a crime, presents or receives money or something else as prepayment or payment for the crime or who procures, constructs, gives, receives, keeps, conveys or engages in any other such activity with poison, explosive, weapon, picklock, falsification tool or other such auxiliary means, shall, in cases where specific provisions have been made governing this, be sentenced for preparation of the crime, unless he is punishable for completed crime or attempt.

In specially designated cases punishment for conspiracy shall also be imposed. By conspiracy is meant that some one decides on the act in concert with another, or also that some one seeks to incite another or agrees to or offers to commit it.

Punishment for preparation or conspiracy shall be fixed lower than the highest and may be fixed below the lowest limit applicable to a completed crime. No greater punishment than imprisonment for two years may be imposed, unless imprisonment for eight or more years may be imposed for the completed crime. If there was slight danger of the crime being completed, no punishment shall be given.

Sec. 3. Punishment for attempt, preparation or conspiracy to commit a crime shall not be imposed on one who voluntarily, by discontinuing the execution of the crime or otherwise, has prevented the completion of the crime. Even though the crime was completed, a person who has unlawfully had to do with auxiliary means may not be punished for that reason if he has voluntarily prevented the criminal use of the means.

Sec. 4. Punishment provided in this Code for an act shall be inflicted not only on the one who committed the act but also on any one who furthered it by advice or deed. A person who is not regarded as the actor shall, if he induced another to commit the act, be punished for instigation of the crime or else for being an accessory to the crime.

Each accomplice shall be judged according to the intent or the carelessness attributable to him. Punishment fixed by law for the act of a manager, debtor or other person in a special position shall also befall a person who together with him was an accomplice in the act.

The provisions of this paragraph do not apply if the law provides otherwise in special cases.

Sec. 5. If some one has been induced to be an accessory to a crime by coercion, deceit or misuse of his youth, lack of comprehension or dependent status or has been an accessory only to a small degree, his punishment may be fixed below that otherwise established for the crime; in trifling cases no punishment shall be imposed. The same applies when it is a question of imposing the punishment established by law for a person in a special position on some other accomplice.

Sec. 6. If a person omits in time to report or otherwise reveal a crime that is occurring, when it can be done without danger to himself or any one of his next of kin, he shall in the cases where this has been covered by special provisions be sentenced for failure to reveal the crime as provided for a person who has been an accessory to the crime only to a smaller degree; however, in no case may a heavier punishment that imprisonment for two years be imposed. In the cases covered by special provisions punishment for failure to reveal a crime as just stated shall also be imposed on one who has not but should have realized that crime was being committed.

If, when it can be done without danger to themselves or their next of kin and without reporting to some authority, parents or other preceptors or guardians, in cases other than those mentioned in the first paragraph, fail to prevent one who is in their care or under their control from committing a crime, punishment for failure to prevent the crime shall be imposed as provided in the first paragraph.

Failure to reveal or prevent a crime is not punishable unless the act being committed has progressed so far that punishment can follow.

Sec. 7. Punishment provided in this Code in a case where some one by crime achieves for himself a gain or appropriates something shall also be imposed when some one intentionally provides a gain for or appropriates something for another.

CHAPTER 24

Of Self-Defense and Other Acts of Necessity

Sec. 1. An act committed by a person in self-defense is not punishable.

A person acts in self-defense, who seeks

to avert an actual or imminent criminal attack on person or property;

to compel one, who by force or threat of force or in other ways obstructs the recapture of property when caught in the act;

to prevent some one from unlawfully forcing his way into a room, house, yard or vessel; or

to remove from a room, house, yard or vessel some one who has unlawfully forced, his way in, or, else, if it is dwelling, refuses to leave when ordered to do so,

and all this so long as the act is not obviously unjustifiable considering the nature of the aggression and the importance of its object.

Sec. 2. If a policeman, who is to execute an official duty

is met with or is attacked by force or threat of force, he may for the accomplishment of his task use such force as can be regarded as justifiable in view of the circumstances. The same applies to a sentry or other serviceman or civilian defense personnel during civilian defense preparations, who performs a police task or serves on guard duty or for maintaining order.

If a prisoner or one who is jailed, taken into custody or otherwise deprived of liberty escapes or, by force or threat of force offers resistance or if he otherwise offers resistance to some one who has him in charge and responsible for making him behave, such force as is justifiable in view of the circumstances may be used to prevent the escape or maintain order. If some one who is to be jailed, taken into custody or otherwise deprived of his liberty tries to avoid or impede the one who has to perform the task, force may also be used as just mentioned. The same applies if, in cases referred to in this paragraph, resistance is offered by some one other than previously mentioned.

If some one has the right according to this section to use force, each person who comes to his assistance shall have the same right.

Sec. 3. In case of mutiny or during combat, as well as on occasions when a crime against military discipline imports a special danger, a serviceman may vis-a-vis a subordinate, who shows disobedience, use the force necessary for maintaining military discipline.

In a case referred to here, the provisions of Section 2, third paragraph, shall apply correspondingly.

Sec. 4. A person, who in a case other than one referred to previously in this Chapter acts out of necessity in order to avert danger to life or health, save valuable property or for others reasons, shall also be free from punishment if the act must be considered justifiable in view of the nature of the danger, the harm caused another and the circumstances in general.

Sec. 5. If, in a case referred to in Sections 1-4, some one has used greater force or caused more serious harm than is permissible in each case, he shall nevertheless not be punished, so long as the circumstances were such that he could hardly have stopped to think.

If the act is found to be criminal, a lesser punishment than that fixed for the crime may be imposed.

Sec. 6. An act committed by some one by order of the person to whom he owes obedience shall not lead to punishment for him, if he had to obey the order in view of the nature of the condition of obedience, the character of the act and the circumstances in general.

Part Three

Of Sanctions

CHAPTER 25

Of Fines, etc.

Sec. 1. Fines are imposed in day-fines.

However, if a certain maximum sum of not more than five hundred kronor is specified for a fine or if its amount is to be determined according to a special basis of computation (standardized fine), the fine is imposed directly in money.

Sec. 2. Day-fines are imposed to a number of at least one and at most one hundred and twenty.

A day-fine is fixed in money in an amount of at least two and at most five hundred kronor, depending on what is deemed reasonable in view of the defendant's income, wealth, obligations to dependents, and other economic circumstances. If the offense is petty, the amount of the day-fine may be adjusted accordingly.

Sec. 3. Unless the law states otherwise, the smallest sanction by fine is ten kronor.

Sec. 4. Fines may be used as a collective punishment for several crimes, if fines can follow on each of the crimes.

A collective punishment by fines does not apply to crimes for which the law has provided standardized fines or fines which may not be converted into imprisonment.

Sec. 5. Fines as collective punishment for several crimes are imposed in day-fines if the law provides such fines for any one of the crimes.

As a collective punishment day-fines may be imposed to a number of one hundred and eighty and a fine directly in money to an amount of one thousand kronor.

If a specified minimum fine is provided for any one of the crimes, a lesser fine may not be imposed.

Sec. 6. Unless otherwise prescribed, fines go to the Crown.

If fines are imposed as collective punishment for several crimes and the fine for any one of the crimes is to go elsewhere than to the Crown or be used for a special purpose, the apportionment of the fines shall be ordered depending on circumstances.

Sec. 7. Special provisions govern the recovery of fines.

Unless otherwise provided, unpaid fines shall be converted into imprisonment for at least ten and at most ninety days in conformity with special provisions applying thereto.

Sec. 8. The provisions of Sec. 6, first paragraph, and of Sec. 7 shall correspondingly apply with respect to a monetary penalty which, by decision of a court or other authority, has been imposed on some one in a particular case. With respect to other monetary penalties, the provisions of this Chapter pertaining to fines shall apply.

CHAPTER 26

Of Imprisonment

Sec. 1. According to what is provided for the crime, imprisonment is imposed for a fixed term of not more than ten years, or for life. A fixed term of imprisonment may not be shorter than one month.

Separate legal provisions govern the use of imprisonment as punishment into which fines have been converted.

Sec. 2. Imprisonment may be used as a collective punishment for several crimes if imprisonment can follow on any one of the crimes.

Imprisonment for a fixed term may be set longer than the longest of the maximum terms that can follow on the crimes, but it may not exceed this by more than two years nor surpass the maximum terms added together; in that connection, punishment by fine is considered as corresponding to the imprisonment which would result from the conversion of the fines.

Imprisonment shorter than the longest of the minimum terms may not be imposed.

Sec. 3. If some one has been sentenced to a sanction for a crime defined in this Code and punishable by imprisonment and he, after the sentence has acquired legal force, again commits a crime defined in the Code and punishable by imprisonment for at most six months, imprisonment for at most two years may be imposed for the new crime. If the new crime is punishable by imprisonment for more than six months but at most two years, imprisonment for at most four years may be imposed for the new crime.

Neither a crime which some one has committed before his eighteenth birthday, nor a sentence to a fine or a disciplinary punishment may be made the basis for the augmentation mentioned in the first paragraph.

A foreign sentence may be given the same effect as a Swedish one.

Sec. 4. A person under eighteen years of age may not be sentenced to imprisonment except for very strong reasons.

Imprisonment may be imposed on one over eighteen but not yet twentyone years of age only when the deprivation of liberty is particularly called for in deference to public law-obedience or else when imprisonment is found more appropriate than another sanction.

Life imprisonment may not be imposed for a crime some one committed before reaching eighteen years of age.

Sec. 5. A person sentenced to imprisonment shall, for the execution of the punishment, be committed to a correctional institution. This is the subject of separate legislation.

Sec. 6. A person serving imprisonment for a fixed term may be paroled after having served two-thirds or, where special reasons exist, one-half of the term. However, parole may not be granted before at least four months have been served. As amended, SFS 1965:620, eff. Jan. 1, 1966.

Sec. 7. When a matter of discretionary parole is being investigated, special note shall be taken of the prisoner's conduct during his stay in the institution and his mental attitude at the time the question of his parole arises, his readiness to make compensation for the damage caused by his crime, and the circumstances in which he would find himself upon release. As amended, SFS 1965:620, eff. Jan. 1, 1966.

Sec. 8. If several sentences to imprisonment are being served concurrently, the combined prison terms shall be taken into consideration in applying Section 6. In that connection, punishment into which fines have been converted shall also be regarded as imprisonment.

If, in accord with governing provisions, the period of imprisonment has been extended due to disciplinary punishment, such extension shall not be counted in computing the time for parole, nor may release on parole occur before the conclusion of such punishment.

The period during which the punishment shall be regarded as being administered as a result of a court order referred to in Chapter 33, Section 3, is also counted as time served. As amended, SFS 1965:620, eff. Jan. 1, 1966.

Sec. 9. Questions of parole are investigated by the supervisory board within whose district the correctional institution is located. As amended, SFS 1965:620, eff. Jan. 1, 1966.

Sec. 10. A parole period of at least one and at most three years or, if the balance of the term at the time of release exceeds three years, at most five years, shall be set in the decision granting parole. As amended, SFS 1965:620, eff. Jan. 1, 1966.

Sec. 11. The parolee shall be under supervision during the parole period.

If at the time of release or later it is found that supervision is not needed, it may be decided that no supervision shall take place. As long as the parole period lasts, the parolee may be placed under supervision, when reasons dictate it. Decisions here referred to are made by the supervisory board.

Sec. 12. A supervisory board is in charge of the supervision. The board appoints a parole officer.

If some one other than the protective supervisor attached to the supervisory board has been appointed parole officer, the supervision shall be under the guidance of such supervisor.

Sec. 13. The parolee shall keep the parole officer informed of his residence and employment, appear before him when summoned, and otherwise maintain contact with him in conformity with his instructions.

Sec. 14. During his parole period, the parolee shall lead an orderly and law-abiding life, avoid harmful company, try to support himself according to his ability, and otherwise observe what is required of him by this Code or by directives or instructions issued by its authority. If he has been enjoined to make compensation for damage caused by his crime, he shall meet this obligation to the best of his ability.

Sec. 15. When it is deemed appropriate for promoting the parolee's adaptation in society, special directives, valid for a given period of time or until further notice, shall be issued with respect to what he has to observe during the parole period. Such directive may have reference to place of residence or lodging, use of leisure time, disposal of wages or other resources, all this for a specified period of at most one year at a time; training, employment, or ban on the use of alcoholic beverages. Other analogous directives may also be issued.

When deemed required, the parolee may be directed to submit to medical care, treatment for alcoholism or other care or treatment in or outside a hospital or other similar establishment.

If the parolee has been enjoined to make compensation for damage caused by his crime, directives may be issued governing the time and manner of meeting this obligation.

Sec. 16. Directives in accord with Section 15 shall be issued by the supervisory board.

If so indicated by the parolee's progress and other personal circumstances, the supervisory board may change a directive issued and also issue a new directive.

Sec. 17. Instructions concerning the carrying out of a directive referred to in Section 15 may be given by the parole officer, who may also allow temporary relief and make a promptly required adjustment.

Sec. 18. If the parolee does not comply with what is required of him by this Code or by directives or instructions issued by its authority, the supervisory board, aside from ordering supervision or issuing a directive in accord with Section 15, may, depending on the circumstances,

1. decide that the parolee be given a warning;
2. extend the parole period by at most one year beyond the time fixed at the time of release;
3. order him, under threat of a monetary penalty, to comply with a directive issued.

Sec. 19. If it can be assumed that a parolee, who has ignored his obligations, will not let himself be corrected by a measure referred to in Section 18, the supervisory board may declare the conditionally granted liberty forfeited.

Sec. 20. A decision concerning a measure referred to in Section 18 or 19 may be made even after the expiration of the parole period, if the question has been under consideration by the supervisory board prior thereto. No other measure there mentioned may be decided upon after the expiration of the parole period, unless that period is prolonged in accord with Section 18.

Sec. 21. Concerning the forfeiture of conditionally granted liberty and concerning certain other measures, when the person sentenced to imprisonment is found to have committed another crime, provisions are found in Chapter 34.

Sec. 22. If a question arises of declaring a conditionally granted liberty forfeited or of taking a measure referred to in Section 18, the supervisory board may, if circumstances indicate it, order that the parolee be appropriately detained while awaiting further order.

A person thus detained may not be held longer than a week. However, if strong reasons dictate it, a new order for his detention for at most an additional week may be issued. He may not be retained in detention after the expiration of the parole period.

Sec. 23. If a conditionally granted liberty is declared forfeited the balance of the prison term shall be regarded as a new term with respect to re-parole. If the parolee is not at the same time sentenced to imprisonment for a fixed term, parole may, however, be granted even though the time mentioned in Section 6 has not ended. As amended, SFS 1965:620, eff. Jan. 1, 1966.

Sec. 24. If a conditionally granted liberty can no longer be declared forfeited, the punishment shall be considered fully served when the parole period expires.

CHAPTER 27

Of Conditional Sentence

Sec. 1. A conditional sentence may be given for a crime punishable by imprisonment, if, with particular consideration of the defendant's character and other personal circumstances, there are firm reasons for assuming that supervision or some other more far-reaching measure is not needed to restrain him from further criminality.

A conditional sentence may not be given if, because of the gravity of the crime or for other reason, an obstacle exists with respect to public law-obedience. A conditional sentence may not be used for a crime by a serviceman, unless it is deemed feasible without danger to military discipline and order within the military forces.

Sec. 2. Whether or not fines are provided by law for the crime, at most one hundred and twenty day-fines may be imposed in addition to the conditional sentence, if this is deemed appropriate for the correction of the defendant or out of consideration for public law-obedience.

Sec. 3. A person who receives a conditional sentence shall undergo a probationary period of two years.

The probationary period begins the day the decision of the court in respect to the sanction for the crime, either by declaration of satisfaction with the decision or otherwise, has acquired legal force against the offender.

Sec. 4. During the probationary period the offender shall lead an orderly and law-abiding life, avoid harmful company, and seek to support himself according to his ability.

Sec. 5. If the offender has been enjoined to make compensation for damage caused by his crime, he shall do what he is able to do to meet this obligation. The court may direct that, during the probationary period, he shall seek to meet his obligation to pay damages or a part thereof at times and in a manner indicated in the sentence.

When reasons dictate it, a directive referred to in the first paragraph may be changed or revoked on application by the prosecutor or by the offender.

Sec. 6. If the offender does not comply with what is required of him by the conditional sentence, the court may, if the prosecutor proceeds in the matter before the expiration of the probationary period, depending on circumstances,

1. decide that the offender be given a warning;
2. issue a directive according to Section 5 or change a directive previously issued;
3. extend the probationary period to three years;

4. vacate the conditional sentence and fix another sanction for the crime.

Unless the probationary period is extended, a measure described in 1 and 2 of the first paragraph may not be taken after the expiration of the probationary period.

If the conditional sentence is vacated, fair consideration shall be given, in deciding on the sanction, to the fine which in accord with Section 2 was imposed in addition to the conditional sentence.

Sec. 7. Concerning the vacating of a conditional sentence and concerning certain other measures, when the offender is found to have committed another crime, provisions are found in Chapter 34.

CHAPTER 28

Of Probation

Sec. 1. If it is deemed necessary that the defendant be placed under supervision and no more far-reaching sanction than probation is needed, a sentence to probation may be imposed for a crime punishable by imprisonment.

A person under eighteen years of age may not be sentenced to probation unless this sanction is deemed more appropriate than care in accord with the Child Welfare Act.

If the mildest punishment provided for the crime is imprisonment for one year or longer, a sentence to probation may be imposed only if strong reasons dictate it.

Sec. 2. Whether or not fines are provided by law for the crime, at most one hundred and twenty day-fines may be imposed in addition to probation, if this is deemed appropriate for the correction of the defendant or out of consideration for public law-obedience.

Sec. 3. If the defendant is eighteen years of age or older, the court may, if it is deemed necessary for his correction or for some other reason, order that the probation shall include treatment in an institution. Such treatment shall continue for at least one and at most two months depending on decisions made as it progresses. In other respects, the treatment is governed by special legislation.

If the probationer has not reached his twenty-third year of age, the court may decide that the order mentioned in the first paragraph shall take effect even though the sentence to probation has not acquired legal force.

Sec. 4. Probation shall last three years.

The probation term begins the day the decision of the court in respect to the sanction for the crime either by declaration of satisfaction with the decision or otherwise, has acquired legal force against the probationer.

If the court has rendered a decision mentioned in Section 3, second paragraph, the probation term shall begin the day of the sentence.

Sec. 5. The probationer shall remain under supervision during his probation term.

When supervision is no longer deemed needed, it shall be ordered terminated. As long as the probation term lasts, the probationer may be placed under supervision anew, if reasons dictate it. A decision here referred to is rendered by the supervisory board.

Sec. 6. Provisions of Chapter 26, Sections 12–17, shall correspondingly apply to a person sentenced to probation. A probation officer may also be assigned and directives based on Chapter 26, Section 15, issued by the court when sentencing to probation.

Sec. 7. If the probationer does not comply with what is required of him in consequence of the sentence to probation, the supervisory board may, aside from ordering placement under supervision or the issuing of a directive in accord with Chapter 26, Section 15, depending on circumstances,

1. decide that the probationer be given a warning;
2. extend the probation term to at most five years;
3. order him, under threat of a monetary penalty, to comply with a directive issued.

A measure referred to in this Section may not be taken by a supervisory board after the expiration of the probation term.

Sec. 8. If the probationer has ignored his obligations and it can be assumed that he will not let himself be corrected by a measure which the supervisory board may take, the board shall ask the prosecutor to raise with the court the question of revoking the probation or of treatment referred to in section 3.

The proceeding just mentioned shall be instituted before the expiration of the probation term.

Sec. 9. If probation is revoked, the court shall import another sanction for the crime. In so doing, fair consideration shall be given to what the probationer has suffered in consequence of the sentence to probation as well as to fines imposed in addition to probation in accord with Section 2; and the court may impose imprisonment for a shorter time than that provided for the crime.

If adequate reasons for the revocation of probation are not present, the court may instead take a measure referred to in Section 7 or, if the probationer is eighteen years of age or older, order that he undergo treatment in accord with Section 3. If the question of such treatment is raised, a decision to revoke probation or to take a measure referred to in Section 7 may be made instead. No other measure than one there mentioned may be ordered when the probation term has expired, unless the term is extended in accord with Section 7.

Sec. 10. Concerning the revocation of probation and concerning certain other measures, when the probationer is found to have committed another crime, provisions are found in Chapter 34.

Sec. 11. If a question arises concerning the revocation of probation or concerning treatment in accord with Section 3 or a measure referred to in Section 7, the supervisory board or the court before which a proceeding has been instituted in accord with Section 8 may, if circumstances dictate it, order the probationer appropriately detained while awaiting further order.

A probationer thus detained may not be held longer than a week. However, if strong reasons dictate it, a new order for his detention for at most an additional week may be issued. He may not be held in detention after the expiration of the probation term.

CHAPTER 29

Of Youth Imprisonment

Sec. 1. A sentence to youth imprisonment may, for a crime punishable by imprisonment, be imposed on a person who is eighteen but not yet twenty-one years of age, if the nurture and training which youth imprisonment is meant to give are deemed appropriate in view of the youth's personal development, conduct and other circumstances.

A person who is not yet eighteen or who is twenty-one but not yet twenty-three years of age may be sentenced to youth imprisonment, if such sanction is deemed obviously more appropriate than another sanction.

The court may order a sentence to youth imprisonment executed even though it has not acquired legal force.

Sec. 2. The treatment of one sentenced to youth imprisonment takes place within or outside an institution and may last for at most five years, of which at most three in an institution.

Sec. 3. The treatment shall begin in an institution.

The institutional care shall be given in a youth institution or, if special reasons dictate it, in some other correctional institution.

Special legislation governs institutional care.

Sec. 4. The treatment shall continue outside the institution when institutional care has lasted as long as needed in view of the aim of the treatment. Unless special reasons dictate it, the youth may not be transferred to care outside the institution before a year has passed since his commitment to the institution.

Sec. 5. The decision on transfer to care outside the institution is rendered by the youth imprisonment board, which may, however, charge the supervisory board in the district in which the institution is located with fixing more precisely the date of the transfer.

If the supervisory board finds that the youth should be transferred to care outside the institution or if he himself applies for such transfer, the board shall refer the matter, together with its own views thereon, to the youth imprisonment board for investigation.

Sec. 6. The youth shall be under supervision during treatment outside the institution.

Sec. 7. With respect to care outside the institution, the provisions of Chapter 26, Sections 12–17, shall have corresponding application. A parole officer may also be assigned and directives in accord with Chapter 26, Section 15, issued by the youth imprisonment board when it orders care outside the institution.

Sec. 8. If a youth under care outside the institution does not comply with what is required of him by this Code or in accord with directives or instructions issued by its authority, the supervisory board, aside from issuing a directive in accord with Chapter 26, Section 15, may, depending on circumstances, decide that he be given a warning, as well as requiring him, under threat of a monetary penalty, to observe a directive issued.

Sec. 9. If a youth under care outside the institution obstinately refuses to meet his obligations or if it is found that because of his conduct or for other reasons institutional care is needed to prevent him from committing crime, the youth imprisonment board may order his re-commitment to the institution.

A re-committed youth shall be again transferred to care outside the institution, when the aim of his treatment is best achieved thereby.

Sec. 10. Concerning re-commitment to an institution and concerning certain other measures, when the youth is found to have committed another crime, provisions are found in Chapter 34.

Sec. 11. If a question arises of recommitting a youth to an institution or of taking a measure referred to in Section 8, the supervisory board or the youth imprisonment board may, if circumstances dictate it, order him appropriately detained while awaiting further order.

A youth thus detained may not be held longer than a week. However, if strong reasons dictate it, a new order for his detention for at most an additional week may be issued. He may not be held in detention after the expiration of the imposed sanction.

Sec. 12. If the need to continue supervision over a youth

under care outside the institution no longer exists, the youth imprisonment board shall order the imposed sanction terminated. Unless special reasons dictate it, however, such order may not be issued until the care outside the institution has lasted two uninterrupted years.

If no order mentioned in the first paragraph is issued, the sanction terminates at the expiration of the maximum length of time the treatment can be given.

CHAPTER 30

Of Internment

Sec. 1. A sentence to internment may be imposed if the crime or, when several crimes have been committed any one of them is punishable by imprisonment for two years or longer and, in view of the defendant's criminality, mental condition, conduct and other circumstances, a long-lasting deprivation of liberty, without duration fixed in advance, is deemed needed to prevent further serious criminality on his part.

Sec. 2. The treatment of a person sentenced to internment takes place within and outside an institution and shall begin in an institution.

Sec. 3. When internment is imposed, the court, in considering the nature of the crime and other circumstances, shall fix a given minimum time of at least one and at most twelve years for custodial institutional care.

Sec. 4. The institutional care shall take place in an internment institution or, if special reasons dictate it, in some other correctional institution.

Special legislation governs the institutional care.

Sec. 5. After the expiration of the minimum term, the treatment shall continue outside the institution, when institutional care is no longer deemed needed to restrain the internee from further criminality.

Sec. 6. The decision on transfer to care outside the institution is rendered by the internment board, which, however, may charge the supervisory board in the district in which the institution is located with fixing more precisely the date of the transfer.

Before the expiration of the minimum term and at least every six months thereafter, the supervisory board shall consider the question of transfer to care outside the institution.

If the supervisory board finds that the internee should be transferred to care outside the institution or if he himself applies for such transfer, the board shall refer the matter, together with its own views thereon, to the internment board for investigation.

Sec. 7. If it is found that the person convicted is in actual need of institutional care and if such care is provided for him after the expiration of the minimum period under the Law on Provision of Closed Psychiatric Care in Certain Cases of Section 35 of the Law Concerning the Treatment of Certain Mentally Disturbed Individuals, the internment board may direct that the internment be terminated. As amended, SFS 1965:295, eff. January 1, 1967 and SFS 1967:942, eff. July 1, 1968.

Sec. 8. Without the consent of the court, care in the institution may not exceed the minimum term by more than three years altogether, or five years altogether, if the minimum term is three years or longer.

The consent referred to in the first paragraph shall be given if it is deemed necessary to prevent further serious criminality on the part of the internee. The consent shall apply to an extension by three years; the term can be further extended, three years at a time, by a new consent.

The proceeding concerning extension is instituted by the attorney general when proposed by the internment board. If such proceeding is instituted, the internee may be held in the institution until the court's decision has acquired legal force.

Sec. 9. The internee shall be under supervision during treatment outside the institution.

Sec. 10. With respect to the care outside the institution, the provisions of Chapter 26, Sections 12–17, shall have corresponding application. A parole officer may also be assigned and directives in accord with Chapter 26, Section 15, issued by the internment board when it orders care outside the institution.

Sec. 11. If an internee under care outside the institution does not comply with what is required of him by this Code or in accord with directives or instructions issued by its authority, the supervisory board, aside from issuing a directive in accord with Chapter 26, Section 15, may, depending on circumstances, decide that he be given a warning, as well as requiring him, under threat of a monetary penalty, to observe a directive issued.

Sec. 12. If an internee under care outside the institution obstinately refuses to meet his obligations or if it is found that because of his conduct or for other reasons institutional care is needed to prevent him from committing crime, the internment board may order his re-commitment to the institution.

A re-committed internee shall again be transferred to care outside the institution when institutional care is no longer deemed necessary.

Sec. 13. Concerning re-commitment to an institution and concerning certain other measures, when the internee is found to have committed another crime, provisions are found in Chapter 34.

Sec. 14. If a question arises of recommitting an internee to an institution or of taking a measure referred to in Section 11, the supervisory board or the internment board may, if circumstances dictate it, order him appropriately detained while awaiting further order.

An internee thus detained may not be held longer than a week. However, if strong reasons dictate it, a new order for his detention for at most an additional week may be issued. He may not be held in detention after the expiration of the imposed sanction.

Sec. 15. If there is no longer a need to continue supervision over an internee under care outside the institution, the internment board shall order the imposed sanction terminated. Unless special reasons dictate it, such an order may not be given before three years have passed since the internee was last transferred to care outside the institution.

If the internee has been under supervision during an uninterrupted period of three years, the board shall consider the possibility of terminating the sanction; if the supervision has lasted five years, the sanction shall be terminated.

CHAPTER 31

Of Surrender for Special Care

Sec. 1. If a person who has committed a criminal act can be subject to *care in accord with the Child Welfare Act,* the court may, after hearing the child welfare board or, in case a pupil in a youth welfare school is involved, the school administration, leave to the board or the administration to arrange for requisite care.

If deemed needed for the correction of the offender or out of consideration for public law-obedience, at most one hundred and twenty day-fines may be imposed in addition to the surrender for care in accord with the Child Welfare Act, whether the law provides fines for the crime or not.

Sec. 2. If a person who has committed a criminal act can be subject to *care in accord with the Temperance Act* by supervision or compulsory commitment to a treatment institution, the court may, after hearing the temperance board or, in case an inmate of such an institution is involved, the institutional administration, leave to the board or the administration to arrange for requisite care.

If a more severe punishment than imprisonment for six months is provided for the crime, surrender for care according to the Temperance Act may take place only if special reasons dictate it.

Sec. 3. If a person who has committed a criminal offense can be provided with care under the Law on the Provision of Closed Psychiatric Care in Certain Cases or care in a mental hospital under Section 35 of the Law Concerning the Treatment of Certain Mentally Disturbed Individuals, the court may, if it finds the need for such care established, order his surrender for mandatory care at an institution for the mentally ill or an institution for the feebleminded. If the act was not committed under the influence of mental disease, feeblemindedness or other mental abnormality of such profound nature that it must be considered equivalent to mental disease, such order may, however, be made only if special reasons dictate it. As amended, SFS 1965:295, eff. January 1, 1967 and SFS 1967:942, eff. July 1, 1968.

Sec. 4. If some one who has committed a criminal act is in need of psychiatric care or supervision and no order based on Section 3 is made, the court may order him surrendered for *open psychiatric care* if, for special reasons, no more far-reaching measure is deemed required.

CHAPTER 32

Of Punishments of Public Servants and Of Disciplinary Punishments of Servicemen

Sec. 1. Suspension involves the loss of a given office for a specific period and is accompanied, during the period the offender is by his sentence deprived of the exercise of his functions, by the loss of the rights and privileges pertaining to the office, unless otherwise provided with respect to some particular right or privilege.

Sec. 2. The period of suspension is fixed at not less than one month and no more than one year, whether the sanction applies to one or to several crimes.

Suspension may be used as collective sanction for several crimes, if each and all of them can incur suspension.

Sec. 3. Suspension may not be enforced while the offender is an inmate undergoing a sanction in a correctional institution or a military jail.

Sec. 4. Dismissal from a given office involves the loss of the office and of the rights and privileges pertaining thereto, unless otherwise provided with respect to some particular right or privilege.

Sec. 5. Dismissal may be used as collective punishment for several crimes for which public servants are punishable, if dismissal can follow upon any one of the crimes.

Sec. 6. Disciplinary punishments for servicemen are arrest and disciplinary fine.

Arrest shall be imposed for at least three and at most thirty days. The sentence is served in a military jail.

A disciplinary fine consists of a deduction from wages or a corresponding cash payment in accord with special legal provisions and is imposed for at least one and at most twenty days.

Sec. 7. Concerning disciplinary punishment as collective punishment for several crimes and, when a crime by a serviceman is involved, concerning sentence to disciplinary punishment instead of to fines and to fines instead of to disciplinary punishment, provisions are found in a special statute, which also contains provisions on the administration of disciplinary punishments.

If a person who is not a serviceman has become punishable for being an accessory to a crime subject to disciplinary punishment, the determination of the sanction shall be made as if day fines instead of disciplinary punishment were provided.

CHAPTER 33

Of Reduction and Exclusion of Sanctions

Sec. 1. No one may be sentenced to a sanction for a crime he committed before he reached fifteen years of age.

Sec. 2. For a crime which some one has committed under the influence of mental disease, feeblemindedness or other mental abnormality of such profound nature that it must be considered equivalent to mental disease, no other sanction may be applied than surrender for special care or, in cases specified in the second paragraph, fine or probation.

Fines may be imposed if they are found answering the purpose of deterring the defendant from further criminality. Probation may be imposed if in view of the circumstances such sanction is considered more appropriate than special care; in such case treatment provided for in Chapter 28, Section 3, may not be prescribed.

The defendant shall be free of sanctions if it is found that a sanction mentioned in this Section should not be imposed.

Sec. 3. If some one is sentenced to imprisonment for a fixed term, fines, suspension or disciplinary punishment in a case for which he has been detained in jail, it may be decided, if deemed reasonable in view of the circumstances, that the sentence shall be considered as having been wholly or partly served by such detention of the defendant.

If some one, who has begun to undergo youth imprisonment, internment or, subsequent to a sentence to probation, treatment provided by Chapter 28, Section 3, is instead sentenced to a punishment mentioned in the first paragraph, it may be decided, if deemed reasonable in view of the circumstances, that the sentence shall be considered as having been wholly or partly served by such institutional care or treatment.

A decision on a matter referred to in this Section may be changed by a higher court when considering an appeal of the sanction imposed, even though the decision was not appealed.

Sec. 4. If some one has committed a crime before reaching the age of eighteen, a milder punishment than that provided for the crime may be imposed, depending on circumstances. If special reasons dictate it, a milder punishment may also be imposed for crime which some one committed under the influence of mental abnormality.

If very strong reasons dictate it and no obvious obstacle exists with reference to public law-obedience, a milder punishment than that provided for the crime may be imposed in other cases as well.

A sanction may be completely dispensed with, if because of special circumstances it is found obvious that no sanction for the crime is necessary.

CHAPTER 34

Certain Provisions Concerning Concurrence of Crimes and Change of Sanction

Sec. 1. If a person who has been sentenced for crime to imprisonment, conditional sentence, probation, youth imprisonment or internment is found to have committed another crime prior to the sentence, or if he commits a new crime subsequent to the sentence but before the sanction has been fully served or otherwise terminated, the court may, depending on circumstances and taking note of what Sections 2–9 prescribe in certain cases,

1. order that the sanction imposed earlier shall apply also to the second crime;
2. impose a separate sanction for that crime, or,
3. if the earlier sentence has acquired legal force, vacate the sanction imposed and impose a different kind of sanction for the crimes.

Sec. 2. If the offender is serving life imprisonment, only an order in accord with Section 1 (1) may be made.

Sec. 3. If the prior sentence is to imprisonment for a fixed term, an order in accord with Section 1 (1) may be made only if it is obvious that, so far as the sanction is concerned, the new crime, compared with the earlier one, is of no importance worth mentioning, or else that strong reasons dictate it.

If in applying Section 1 (2) punishment is imposed for crime committed before the execution of the earlier sentence has begun, possible care should be taken in determinimg the punishment that the combined punishments do not exceed what could have been imposed for the two crimes in accord with Chapter 26, Section 2, and in so doing a milder punishment than that provided for the crime may be imposed.

The vacating of imprisonment in conformity with Section 1 (3) may occur only if sentence is pronounced before the prison term has been fully served.

Sec. 4. If Section 1 (1) or (2) is applied with respect to some one paroled from imprisonment, the conditionally granted liberty may be declared forfeited; if a fixed term of imprisonment is imposed in conformity with Section 1 (2), such declaration shall be made, unless special reasons oppose it.

If forfeiture in accord with the first paragraph is not ordered, the court may decide on a measure referred to in Chapter 26, Section 18.

Forfeiture or a measure just mentioned may not be decided unless the question concerning it is raised in a case in which the parolee has been committed to jail or been informed of the prosecution before the expiration of the parole term.

Sec. 5. If the sanction previously imposed is a conditional sentence, an order based on Section 1 (1) may have reference only to a crime committed before the beginning of the probationary period.

If Section 1 (1) or (2) is applied, the court may decide on a measure mentioned in Chapter 27, Section 6 (1–3), but only if the question concerning it is raised in a case in which the offender has been committed to jail or been informed of the prosecution before the expiration of the probationary period.

The vacating of a conditional sentence in conformity with Section 1 (3) may not take place unless the question concerning it is raised in a case in which the offender has been committed to jail or been informed of the prosecution within a year from the expiration of the probationary period.

Sec. 6. If the sanction previously imposed is probation, the court may, in applying Section 1 (1) or (2), decide on a measure or treatment referred to in Chapter 28, Section 9.

If in applying Section 1 (3) imprisonment is imposed, the provisions of Chapter 28, Section 9, shall govern the determination of the punishment.

A decision in accord with the first paragraph or a decision revoking probation may not be taken unless the question concerning it is raised in a case in which the offender has been committed to jail or been informed of the prosecution before the expiration of the probationary period.

Sec. 7. If the sanction previously imposed is youth imprisonment, an order according to Section 1 (1) may be made in disregard of what Chapter 29, Section 1, states concerning the age of the defendant.

If the offender is under care in an institution, the provision of Section 1 (2) may not be applied.

The vacating of youth imprisonment in conformity with Section 1 (3) may occur only if sentence is passed before the sanction is terminated. If, in applying Section 1 (3), a sentence to imprisonment is imposed, fair consideration shall be given, when determining the punishment, to what the offender has suffered on account of the earlier sentence, and in that connection imprisonment may be imposed for a shorter time than indicated in Chapter 26, Section 2.

Sec. 8. If Section 1 (1) or (2) is applied to one sentenced to youth imprisonment, the court may extend the maximum term of such imprisonment to six years, in which case treatment in an institution may take place for at most four years.

If in accord with Section 1 (1) the order is made that youth imprisonment shall apply to another crime as well, the court may decide that the youth shall be re-committed to an institution. If the crime was committed after the execution of the sentence to youth imprisonment had begun, the court may also direct that one who is under care in an institution or is being re-committed may not be transferred to care outside the institution before six months have elapsed from the date of the court's decision or the re-commitment, so long as the maximum period for care in the institution does not expire earlier.

A decision referred to in this Section may not be made unless the question concerning it is raised in a case in which the offender has been committed to jail or been informed of the prosecution before the sanction has terminated.

Sec. 9. If the sanction previously imposed is internment and the internee is under care outside the institution, the court, when applying Section 1 (1), may decide that he shall be re-committed to the institution. If such decision is made or if Section 1 (1) is applied in the case of one under care in an institution, the court shall, unless special reasons oppose it, fix a minimum term for the institutional care in progress. In such case the minimum time fixed shall be at least six months.

If the offender is under care in an institution, the provision of Section 1 (2) may not be applied.

The vacating of internment in conformity with Section 1 (3) may occur only if sentence is passed before the sanction has terminated. If imprisonment is imposed, the provisions of Section 7, third paragraph, shall have corresponding application.

Sec. 10. If on the basis of Section 1 (1) a sentence which has acquired legal force has directed that imprisonment, conditional sentence, probation youth imprisonment or internment imposed in an earlier case shall cover further crime, and if the earlier sentence is changed by a higher court by a judgment which acquires legal force, the question of sanction for said crime shall, upon notification by the prosecutor, be reconsidered by the court. The same shall apply when a punishment has been decided on the basis of Section 3, second paragraph, and the punishment imposed earlier is changed.

If, when a sentence to imprisonment for a fixed term is to be executed, it is found that the offender committed the crime before the execution of such punishment, imposed on him for another crime, has begun, and if it does not appear from the sentences that the other punishment has been taken into consideration, the court, once the sentences have acquired legal force, shall, upon notification by the prosecutor and on the basis of Section 3, second paragraph, fix the punishment the offender shall suffer as a result of the sentence which is to be executed last.

Sec. 11. If the execution of a sentence to life imprisonment is to take place concurrently with a sentence to a fine, punishment to which a fine has been converted, imprisonment for a fixed term, conditional sentence, probation, youth imprisonment, internment or disciplinary punishment, the life sentence shall supplant the other sanction.

Sec. 12. If the execution of a sentence to youth imprisonment is to take place concurrently with a sentence to a fine, punishment to which a fine has been converted, imprisonment for at most one year, conditional sentence, probation or disciplinary punishment, the sentence to youth imprisonment shall supplant the other sanction, if the youth is to be under care in an institution while serving his sentence.

If the execution of a sentence to youth imprisonment is to occur concurrently with a sentence to imprisonment for a fixed term of more than one year, the prosecutor shall, when the sentences have acquired legal force, notify the court. Depending on circumstances, the court may declare that one of the sanctions shall supplant the other or may vacate the sentence to youth imprisonment and impose a sentence to imprisonment for the crime or crimes involved. If the court sentences to imprisonment, Section 7, third paragraph, shall apply.

Sec. 13. If the execution of a sentence to internment is to occur concurrently with a sentence to a fine, punishment into which a fine has been converted, imprisonment for a fixed term, conditional sentence, probation, youth imprisonment or disciplinary punishment, the internment shall supplant the other sanction, if the offender is to be under care in an institution while serving his sentence.

If, in view of the nature of the additional crime, which the internment is thus to cover, a new minimum term for the institutional care is deemed needed, the court may fix such term upon application by the prosecutor.

Sec. 14. If some one has been sentenced to suspension from a given office and, before sentence or later before the execution of the sentence has begun, he is found to have committed another crime, for which he shall be suspended from the same office, the court may, depending on circumstances,

1. declare that the sentence to suspension already imposed shall cover the other crime as well, or

2. sentence to suspension for such crime separately, in which case the combined time of the punishment may not exceed one year.

Sec. 15. Provisions of Section 10 shall correspondingly apply in a matter of suspension; however, instead of Section 3, second paragraph, the provisions of Section 14 (2) shall govern.

Sec. 16. If some one has been sentenced to dismissal from a given office and it is found that before the sentence acquired legal force he had committed another crime for which he should have been sentenced to suspension or dismissal from the same office, the court shall declare that the sentence to dismissal shall cover the other crime as well.

Sec. 17. Fine or disciplinary punishment may not be imposed for a crime defined in Chapter 20, Sections 1–4, when a sentence of suspension or dismissal is imposed for another crime and such punishment is deemed sufficient.

CHAPTER 35

Of Limitations on Sanctions

Sec. 1. No sanction may be imposed unless the suspect has been committed to jail or informed of his prosecution for the crime within

1. two years, if the crime is punishable by no more severe punishment than imprisonment for one year;
2. five years, if the most severe punishment is imprisonment for more than one but not longer than two years;
3. ten years, if the most severe punishment is imprisonment for more than two but no longer than eight years;
4. fifteen years, if the most severe punishment is imprisonment for a fixed term of more than eight years;
5. twenty-five years, if the crime is punishable by life imprisonment.

If an act includes several crimes, a sanction may be imposed for all the crimes, regardless of what has just been stated, so long as a sanction can be imposed for any one of them.

Sec. 2. A sanction may not be imposed for a crime defined in Chapter 20, Sections 1–4, unless the suspect has been committed to jail or been informed of his prosecution for the crime within five years or, if the crime is punishable as mentioned in Section 1 (3) above, within the time there stated.

Sec. 3. If a person committed to jail is released without having been informed of his prosecution for the crime or if the case against him is dismissed or filed after he has been so informed, the commitment or information shall be considered as never having occurred, if a question of the possibility of imposing a sanction is raised.

Sec. 4. The times specified in Sections 1 and 2 shall be counted from the date the crime was committed. If the appearance of a given consequence of the act is a prerequisite for the imposition of a sanction, the time shall be counted from the date such consequence appeared.

In cases referred to in Chapter 7, Section 2, the time shall be counted from the date the sentence of annulment of the marriage acquired legal force, and in the case referred to in Chapter 11, Section 5, from the date the decision concerning the alienation of property was given or else the earliest date prosecution could be instituted.

Sec. 5. Repealed, SFS 1971:964, eff. Jan. 1, 1972.

Sec. 6. In no case may a sanction be imposed when, from the date mentioned in Section 4, the following periods have elapsed:

1. five years, if the crime is not punishable by more than

a fine and the time for the imposition of a sanction for the crime is determined under Section 1 (1),

2. fifteen years, if other than under paragraph 1 the crime is not punishable by imprisonment for more than two years,

3. thirty years in other cases. As amended, SFS 1971:964, eff. January 1, 1972.

Sec. 7. Fines imposed are null and void when three years have elapsed from the date the sentence acquired legal force, if before such time no application for the conversion of the fines has been brought to the notice of the offender. Special provisions exist concerning the nullification of fines when such notification has been made and of imprisonment into which fines have been converted.

If the offender dies, imposed fines are nullified. If the sentence acquired legal force during the offender's lifetime and if in satisfaction of the fines chattel property has been distrained or placed in public custody, the fines shall, however, be payable out of such property.

What has been said now about fines, applies equally to a monetary penalty ordered paid.

Sec. 8. A sentence to imprisonment is null and void if its execution has not begun before the period stated below has elapsed since the sentence acquired legal force:

1. five years, if imprisonment for not more than one year was imposed;

2. ten years, if imprisonment for a period in excess of one year but not more than four years was imposed;

3. fifteen years, if imprisonment in excess of four years but not over eight years was imposed;

4. twenty years, if imprisonment for a fixed term longer than eight years had been imposed;

5. thirty years, if life imprisonment had been imposed. As amended, SFS 1971:964, eff. January 1, 1972.

Sec. 9. If the serving of a sentence to imprisonment for a fixed term is interrupted, the provisions in Section 8 shall correspondingly apply with respect to the continuation of the serving of the sentence; in such case the time shall be computed with consideration of what remains of the punishment imposed. The time shall be counted from the date the interruption occurred or, when parole has been granted but declared revoked, from the date the declaration acquired legal force.

Sec. 10. Unless the execution of the sentence has already begun, a sentence to youth imprisonment is null and void when five years have elapsed, and a sentence to internment when fifteen years have elapsed since the sentence acquired legal force.

If the serving of a sentence to youth imprisonment or internment is interrupted while the offender is under care in an institution, or if a decision to re-commit him to the institution is taken while he is under care outside the institution, the provision of the first paragraph shall correspondingly apply with regard to the continuation of the serving of the sentence; in such case, the time shall be counted from the date of the interruption or the date the re-commitment order acquired legal force.

Sec. 11. Special legislation governs the nullification of disciplinary punishments.

CHAPTER 36

Of Forfeiture of Property and Of Other Special Legal Effects of Crime

Sec. 1. The profits of a crime under this Code which do not correspond to injury to the individual shall be declared forfeited if this is not obviously unreasonable. The same shall apply to a bribe for a crime or its value if the bribe was accepted and the recipient committed a crime under this Code. As amended, SFS 1968:165, eff. July 1, 1968.

Sec. 2. Property which has been used as an instrument in the commission of a crime under this Code or which is the product of such a crime may be declared forfeited if this is called for in order to prevent crime or for other special reasons. The same shall apply to property the use of which constitutes a crime under this Code or which is otherwise used in a manner which constitutes such a crime.

The value of property may be declared forfeited instead of the property itself. As amended, SFS 1968:165, eff. July 1, 1968.

Sec. 3. An object which because of its special character and other circumstances raises an apprehension that it may be put to criminal use, may be declared forfeited even in cases other than those covered in Sec. 2. As amended, SFS 1968:165, eff. July 1, 1968.

Sec. 4. Forfeiture of property or its worth on account of crime may (if no provision is otherwise made) be imposed against:

a) the offender or another who participated in the crime;

b) the person whose position was occupied by the offender or other accomplice;

c) the person who profited from the crime;

d) the person who acquired the property after the crime because of marital property rights, inheritance or devise, or through a gift or who acquired the property after the crime in another way and in so doing had knowledge of or reason to assume that the property was connected with the crime.

If the property did not belong to any of the persons categorized in a)–c), it may not be declared forfeited.

Special right to property which has been declared forfeited remains if the special right is not also declared to be forfeited. As amended, SFS 1968:165, eff. July 1, 1968.

Sec. 5. Instead of forfeiture, the court may prescribe a measure in order to prevent misusage.

Sec. 6. Provisions in law or statute with regard to a special legal effect of some one's being sentenced to punishment shall apply also when some other sanction mentioned in Chapter 1, Section 3, is imposed.

In applying the first paragraph, conditional sentence, probation, youth imprisonment and internment, and also, unless the sentence otherwise states, surrender for special care shall be considered equivalent to imprisonment. In that connection, internment and, if so ordered, probation, youth imprisonment and surrender for special care shall be considered as corresponding to imprisonment for at least six months.

Sec. 7. If sentencing some one to a sanction is prerequisite to the forfeiture of property or other special legal effect, which can follow upon crime, the court may, if the sanction for the crime is remitted, order, in so far as circumstances dictate it, that such legal effect shall ensue.

Sec. 8. If a crime has been committed by some one who has not reached fifteen years of age or who has acted under the influence of mental disease, feeblemindedness or other mental abnormality of such profound nature that it must be considered as equivalent to mental disease, the court may order forfeiture of property or other special legal effect that can follow upon the crime only if and to the extent this can be regarded as reasonable in view of his mentality, the nature of the act, and other circumstances.

Sec. 9. If a sanction can no longer be imposed because of the death of the criminal or for other cause, property may be declared forfeited because of the crime or measure imposed to avert misuse only if, in a proceeding pertaining thereto, a summons has been served within five years from the time the crime was committed. In such a case the prosecutor may institute proceedings only if deemed required in the public interest.

In a case just mentioned, the provisions of Chapter 35, Section 3, shall have corresponding application. As amended, SFS 1968:165, eff. July 1, 1968.

Sec. 10. A decision concerning forfeiture or measure to avert misuse is null and void to the extent that its execution has not occurred within ten years from the date the decision acquired lawful force. As amended, SFS 1968:165, eff. July 1, 1968.

Sec. 11. If a law or statute requires that an explanation be furnished concerning forfeiture or other such special legal consequence of a crime, this may nevertheless be omitted if this legal consequence is obviously unreasonable. Added, SFS 1968:165, eff. July 1, 1968.

Sec. 12. Forfeited property goes to the Crown if nothing is otherwise prescribed. Added, SFS 1968:165, eff. July 1, 1968.

CHAPTER 37

Of Boards

Sec. 1. The area of a supervisory board's activity shall cover the district of one or more public courts of first instance.

However, special supervisory boards may be appointed to deal with matters concerning persons sentenced to imprisonment, youth imprisonment or internment. The area of a supervisory board's activity is determined by the King.

A supervisory board consists of five members, unless the King decrees that a given board shall have more members. The chairman and two members constitute a quorum. In urgent cases as well as in matters of less importance the chairman alone may act on behalf of the board. Such action shall be reported at the next meeting of the board.

The King may order that a supervisory board shall work in sections. Applicable parts of the law governing the board shall apply to such section. As amended, SFS 1966:188, eff. June 9, 1966.

Sec. 2. The King appoints the chairman of the supervisory board and a substitute who, in the absence of the chairman, serves in his stead. When both the chairman and substitute are absent, a temporary substitute is to be appointed by the court of appeals in whose district the supervisory board has its chief area of activity.

Other members and their substitutes are appointed by the county administration in the county within which the supervisory board has its chief area of activity. They should have experience involving youth care or employment agencies or else in public functions.

Members and non-temporary substitutes are appointed for terms of five years. If a member or non-temporary substitute leaves before the expiration of his term, a new member or substitute is appointed to serve for the balance of the term. Temporary substitutes are appointed for six months at most. As amended, SFS 1966:188, eff. June 9, 1966.

Sec. 3. In accord with provisions below there shall be a special board, the board of corrections, for dealing with matters concerning parole. This board shall consist of one member, who occupies or has occupied a judicial office and who shall be chairman of the board, and four additional members. Substitutes are appointed to a number determined by the King. The King appoints the chairman, other members and substitutes. In the absence of the chairman, his function shall be exercised by a member or substitute designated by the King and qualified for appointment as chairman.

The chairman, other members and substitutes are appointed for terms of five years. If a member or substitute leaves before the expiration of his term, a new member or substitute is appointed to serve for the balance of the term.

Sec. 4. The youth imprisonment board and the internment board shall each consist of a member, who occupies or has occupied a judicial office and who shall be chairman of the board, and one member who is a psychiatrist, both of them with special substitutes who have the qualifications required of the respective members, and three additional members together with substitutes to a number determined by the King. The King appoints the chairman, other members and substitutes. In the absence of the chairman, his function shall be exercised by a member or substitute designated by the King and qualified for appointment as chairman.

In urgent cases as well as in matters of less importance, the chairman alone may act on behalf of the board. Such action shall be reported at the next meeting of the board.

The chairman, other members and substitutes are appointed for terms of five years. If a member or substitute leaves before the expiration of his term, a new member or substitute is appointed to serve for the balance of the term.

Sec. 5. A member or substitute of a supervisory board, the board of corrections, the youth imprisonment board and the internment board shall have taken a judge's oath. The same grounds for disqualification that apply to a judge shall apply to a member or substitute, but the provisions of Chapter 4, Section 13 (7) of the Code of Procedure shall not be applicable to a member or substitute of a supervisory board.

With respect to decisions by a board referred to in the first paragraph, applicable parts of the provisions governing voting in criminal cases in a superior court shall be observed.

Sec. 6. If an offender requests a personal appearance in a matter dealt with by a supervisory board, he shall be granted the opportunity.

In a matter before the board of corrections, the youth imprisonment board and the internment board an opportunity for a personal appearance should be granted to the offender if this can be assumed to be useful and can be conveniently arranged. As amended, SFS 1971:570, eff. January 1, 1972.

Sec. 7. A person sentenced to imprisonment may request the board of corrections to review a decision by a supervisory board in a matter of parole.

If a parolee is not satisfied with the supervisory board's decision relative to placement under supervision in accord with Chapter 26, Section 11, a directive in accord with Chapter 26, Section 15, or a measure in accord with Chapter 26, Section 18, 19, or 22, he may request the board of corrections to review the decision.

Sec. 8. A person sentenced to probation may appeal to the circuit court of appeals against a supervisory board's decision relative to placement under supervision in accord with Chapter 28, Section 5, a measure in accord with Chapter 28, Section 7 or 11, or a directive referred to in Chapter 26, Section 15. The time for appeal is counted from the date he was informed of the decision.

Sec. 9. If a person sentenced to youth imprisonment or internment is not satisfied with the decision of the supervisory board in accord with Chapter 29, Section 8 or 11 or Chapter 30, Section 11 or 14, or relative to a directive referred to in Chapter 26, Section 15, he may request the youth imprisonment board or the internment board to review the decision.

Sec. 10. A supervisory board's decision mentioned in Sections 7–9 shall be instantly obeyed unless otherwise provided.

Sec. 11. No appeal may be taken against a decision made by a supervisory board in accord with this Code except in cases mentioned in Sections 7–9; by a circuit court of appeals in accord with Section 8 or by the board of corrections, the youth imprisonment board or the internment board.

CHAPTER 38

Procedural Provisions, etc.

Sec. 1. A person sentenced to conditional sentence or to probation may, before the time for appeal has expired, make a declaration that he is satisfied with the judgment as to the sanction imposed. Such declaration shall also cover fines imposed on the basis of Chapter 27, Section 2, or Chapter 28, Section 2, and includes treatment mentioned in Chapter 28, Section 3. The declaration shall be made in the manner prescribed by the King.

A declaration once made in the prescribed manner is not retractable. If the offender has appealed the sentence, his appeal shall be considered withdrawn by the declaration so far as the sanction for the crime is concerned.

Special provisions exist relating to the declaration of satisfaction in connection with a sentence to imprisonment, youth imprisonment or internment.

Sec. 2. If a court has surrendered some one for care in accord with the Child Welfare Act or the Temperance Act but it is found, upon investigation prescribed, that the prerequisites indicated by law for such care, or for care of the kind the child welfare board or the temperance board declared themselves, in a report to the court, prepared to arrange, are absent, the court which first adjudicated the case may, upon application by the prosecutor, vacate the order for surrender for special care and impose another sanction for the crime.

Sec. 3. A question concerning a measure in accord with Chapter 27, Section 5, second paragraph, or Section 6, is dealt with by the court which first adjudicated the case in which conditional sentence was passed.

A proceeding based on Chapter 28, Section 8, shall be instituted in the public court of first instance, within whose district the supervisory board which is in charge of the supervision of the offender is active.

A proceeding based on Chapter 30, Section 8, is instituted in the court which first adjudicated the case in which internment was imposed.

Cases referred to in this Section may also be brought before a court presently adjudicating a criminal charge against the offender, or before the court in the locality where the offender is mostly staying, if, in view of the investigation as well as costs and other circumstances, the court deems it appropriate.

Sec. 4. Notification based on Chapter 34, Section 10, 12 or 15 is addressed to the first court in any one of the cases.

Application based on Chapter 34, Section 13, is made to

the court which first adjudicated the case in which internment was imposed.

Sec. 5. A proceeding to which reference is made in Chapter 27, Section 6, Chapter 28, Section 8, or Chapter 30, Section 8, shall be considered instituted, when the offender was informed of the opening of the case.

Sec. 6. A board shall participate in a lower court decision on questions referred to in Section 2 or in Chapter 27, Section 6, Chapter 28, Section 9, Chapter 30, Section 8, or Chapter 34, Section 10, second paragraph, 12 or Section 13 or Section 15, insofar as the application of Section 10, second paragraph is concerned. The same shall apply with respect to the vacating of sanctions in accord with Chapter 34, Section 1(3), the forfeiture of conditionally granted liberty or other measure in accord with Chapter 34, Section 4, measure in accord with Chapter 34, Section 5, measure or treatment in accord with Chapter 34, Section 6 as well as re-commitment to an institution or other measure in accord with Chapter 34, Section 8 or 9.

A lower court is competent to decide a question concerned with Chapter 27, Section 5, second paragraph or Chapter 28, Section 11, with one judge who is learned in the law. As amended, SFS 1969:259, eff. January 1, 1970 (SFS 1969:512).

Sec. 7. If a question of sentencing to internment arises, the court shall, unless deemed unnecessary for some special reason, request an opinion from the internment board as to whether or not such a measure should be taken.

Before the court, in accord with Chapter 34, Section 1, decides on a measure concerning some one sentenced to youth imprisonment or internment, an opinion shall, if found needed, be secured from the youth imprisonment board or the internment board. What has now been said shall have corresponding application in cases referred to in Chapter 34, Section 12.

Sec. 8. In a proceeding concerning a measure in accord with Section 2 or Chapter 27, Section 5, second paragraph, or Section 6; Chapter 28, Section 9, Chapter 30, Section 8, or Chapter 34, Section 10, second paragraph, Section 12 or 13 or 15, in so far as the application of Section 10, second paragraph, is concerned, the court of first instance shall give the offender an opportunity to express himself. If he requests to be heard orally, he shall be given the opportunity. The court's adjudication of the matter is by decision.

A measure in accord with Chapter 28, Section 11, may be decided without giving the offender an opportunity to express himself.

Sec. 9. The court's decision on a measure in accord with Chapter 27, Section 5, second paragraph, Chapter 28, Section 11, or Chapter 34, Section 10, second paragraph, Section 12 or 13 or 15, in so far as the application of Section 10, second paragraph, is concerned, is to be instantly obeyed, unless otherwise decided. The same applies to decisions based on Chapter 27, Section 6, Chapter 28, Section 9, or Chapter 34, Section 4, 5, 6 or 8 with reference to directives, monetary penalties, probationary period or length of youth imprisonment.

If a decision in accord with Chapter 28, Section 9, second paragraph, or Chapter 34, Section 6, intends that someone not yet twenty-three years of age is to undergo treatment established by Chapter 28, Section 3, the court may order the decision to be executed even though it has not acquired legal force. Such order may also be given with respect to a decision in accord with Chapter 34, Section 8, concerning re-commitment to an institution of one undergoing youth imprisonment.

Sec. 10. A warning decided upon by a court or a supervisory board shall be promptly delivered to the offender in person. If the warning cannot be delivered in connection with the decision, another court or supervisory board may be requested to deliver it.

Sec. 11. A monetary penalty imposed by authority of Chapter 26, Section 18, Chapter 28, Section 7 or 9, Chapter 29, Section 8, Chapter 30, Section 11, or Chapter 34, Section 4 or 6, may be enforced only if the prosecutor, upon application by the supervisory board, institutes a proceeding in point before the sanction imposed has been fully executed or otherwise terminated. Such proceeding shall be considered instituted when the offender has been informed of the application for enforcement of the monetary penalty.

Sec. 12. It is the duty of police authorities to assist the court, the supervisory board, the board of corrections, the youth imprisonment board and the internment board in assuring the offender's appearance at a proceeding or in a matter dealt with in accord with this Code or in his detention in accord with Chapter 26, Section 22, Chapter 28, Section 11, Chapter 29, Section 11, or Chapter 30, Section 14.

Sec. 13. More detailed directives required for the application of the provisions of Chapters 25–38 are issued by the King.